Praise for *Two Cheers for Minority Government*:

"A wonderful book about parliamentary government in general and minority government in particular. Throughout, Peter Russell maintains his lucid and down-to-earth style of writing and makes an engaging argument for the benefits of minority government. This is one of those rare books that specialists as well as regular folk will benefit from reading."

—*Jennifer Smith, Dalhousie University*

"An insightful and highly readable look at the current state of Canadian parliamentary politics. In an era when minority government may well be here to stay, Professor Russell shows convincingly why Canadians can and should make it work."

—*Larry LeDuc, University of Toronto*

"Professor Russell has demonstrated again why he is one of Canada's most distinguished political scientists. *Two Cheers for Minority Government* is an invaluable citizens' guide that challenges conventional wisdom. Through an examination of minority governments in Canada and around the world, Russell shows they can be capable, effective, and perhaps most importantly, can reinvigorate parliament."

—*Jonathan Rose, Queen's University*

Two Cheers for Minority Government

The Evolution of Canadian Parliamentary Democracy

Peter H. Russell

University of Toronto (Professor Emeritus)

2008
Emond Montgomery Publications Limited
Toronto, Canada

Emond Montgomery Publications Limited
60 Shaftesbury Avenue
Toronto ON M4T 1A3
http://www.emp.ca/university

Printed in Canada.

We acknowledge the financial support of the Government of Canada through the Book Publishing Industry Development Program (BPIDP) for our publishing activities.

Acquisitions and developmental editor: Mike Thompson
Marketing coordinator: Kulsum Merchant
Copy editor: Sarah Gleadow
Proofreader: Claudia Kutchukian
Production editor: Jim Lyons, WordsWorth Communications
Text designer: Tara Wells, WordsWorth Communications
Indexer: Paula Pike, WordsWorth Communications
Cover designers: Stephen Cribbin & Simon Evers
Cover photo: Johannes Singler

Library and Archives Canada Cataloguing in Publication

Russell, Peter H.

Two cheers for minority government : the evolution of Canadian parliamentary democracy / Peter H. Russell.

Includes index.
ISBN 978-1-55239-271-3

1. Representative government and representation—Canada.
2. Democracy—Canada.   3. Coalition governments—Canada.
4. Canada—Politics and government—2006-   I. Title.

JL75.R88 2008   321.8'0430971   C2008-900095-1

To the legacy of Winston Leonard Spencer Churchill,
the greatest parliamentarian of them all

Contents

Acknowledgments

I began thinking seriously about minority government when the President's Circle at the University of Toronto asked me to participate in its annual lecture series in which university professors speak on topics of interest to the general public. The invitation came in the fall of 2004 and Paul Martin's minority government had just come to power. Canadians had not experienced a minority government since Joe Clark's 1979 fiasco. So there was a lot of buzz about this strange and apparently scary political aberration. I thought it was time to look more closely at the phenomenon of minority government, and so chose it as the subject of my University Professor lecture.

That lecture advanced the basic argument of this book—that minority government, far from being a threatening prospect, was a promising opportunity to reverse the illiberal trends of one-party majority governments that were undermining parliamentary democracy in our country. The lecture seemed to go down well when I gave it in the fall of 2004 and subsequently to other current-events groups in Toronto and environs. In 2006, when Stephen Harper's minority government followed Paul Martin's, there was increasing interest in the subject. Like it or not, minority governments seemed likely to be around for a while. So I decided the time was ripe for a book that looked more systematically at what minority governments had done in Canada and elsewhere and at what they could do—if we learned how to make the most of them.

It is doubtful that I would ever have written such a book had I not joined the Churchill Society for the Advancement of Parliamentary Democracy in 1996 and, from 2001 to 2003, served as its Chair. Attending the Society's annual dinner and listening to the winners of its award for Excellence in Advancing Parliamentary Democracy, participating in the Society's many educational activities related to parliamentary democracy, and learning how a lifetime of participation in parliamentary deliberation was at the very core of Winston Churchill's contribution to our freedom—all of this made me aware as I never had been before of the genius of our parliamentary form of democracy and the danger of losing it. I would like to acknowledge here my debt to the founders of the Churchill Society and to its members who have carried forward its work with such dedication. I know they will engage me in argument about what I say in this book. But I know equally well that, being the good Churchillians they are, they will enjoy the engagement.

Parliamentary politics has not been a central part of my work as a political scientist. So I came to the writing of this book as something of a novice. I have benefited greatly from the help and encouragement of colleagues much more learned in the lore of parliamentary democracy than I. In particular, I would like to thank Professors Larry LeDuc and Graham White for their guidance on the literature of parliamentary government and their careful reading of the manuscript. I am also grateful to Elliot Leyton, a fine writer and friend outside of political science, who read the manuscript and offered helpful suggestions. I hasten to add that I am totally responsible for my version of the facts and for the opinions expressed in the book.

I would also like to thank Mike Thompson, acquisitions and developmental editor at Emond Montgomery, for his enthusiastic support of my minority government project and for his help in bringing it to fruition. This is my first book with Emond Montgomery and I found publishing with them a most positive experience. I would particularly like to thank Sarah Gleadow for her very thoughtful and thorough editing of my manuscript.

About the Author

Peter H. Russell is a University Professor Emeritus at the University of Toronto, where he taught political science from 1958 until his retirement in 1996. He is a past president of the Canadian Political Science Association and of the Canadian Law and Society Association. He was the founding president of both RALUT (Retired Academics and Librarians of the University of Toronto) and CURAC (College and University Retiree Associations of Canada). He is a director and past chair of the Churchill Society for the Advancement of Parliamentary Democracy.

Peter Russell has published widely in the fields of constitutional, judicial, and Aboriginal politics. Among his best-known books are *The Judiciary in Canada: The Third Branch of Government*, *Constitutional Odyssey: Can Canadians Become a Sovereign People?* and *Recognizing Aboriginal Title: The Mabo Case and Indigenous Resistance to English Settler Colonialism*. He is an Officer of the Order of Canada and a Fellow of the Royal Society of Canada.

CHAPTER ONE

Introduction

On January 23, 2006, we Canadians elected a new Parliament—Canada's 39th since Confederation. The House of Commons in this Parliament had 125 Conservative, 102 Liberal, 51 Bloc Québécois, 29 NDP, and 1 Independent MP. That, incidentally, is what we Canadians—and the citizens of all parliamentary democracies—do at election time. We don't elect a government; we elect a representative assembly. The government is formed by the leader of the party that has the confidence (that is, the support of a majority of the members) of the elected branch of the legislature—in our federal parliamentary system, the House of Commons.

The day after the election, Paul Martin, the prime minister going into the election, remained the prime minister. That is always the case in parliamentary elections. Remember that, through our votes, we the electorate create a parliament, not a government. Even Kim Campbell remained prime minister for a very short time after the 1993 election in which her Progressive Conservatives garnered only two seats in the 295-seat House of Commons. The day after the election, Prime Minister Campbell called on Governor General Ray Hnatyshyn to tell him whether she intended to carry on as prime minister or resign. Of course, with such a miserable election result, Campbell really had no choice. She offered her resignation and advised his Excellency to call on Jean Chrétien, whose Liberals had a large majority in the newly elected House of Commons, to form a government.

On January 24, 2006, although Paul Martin's Liberals had done much better than Campbell's Progressive Conservatives, Martin's options were really not much better than Campbell's. Theoretically, he could have decided to try his luck with the new House of Commons and see whether he could secure the support of the NDP and enough Bloc members to support a Liberal minority government. But that was surely a most unattractive and unlikely base for governing. So, Prime Minister Martin did the sensible thing. On January 24, he submitted his resignation to Governor General Michaëlle Jean and advised her to call on Stephen Harper, the Conservative leader, to form a government. Mr. Harper did not hesitate to accept Madam Jean's commission.

The government that Mr. Harper formed and that was sworn in on February 6, 2006 was a minority government. With 125 Conservatives in a 308-member House, the Harper government would clearly need the support of other parties to survive. But unlike Martin, whose personal and party fortunes were on the down slope, Harper's and the new Conservative party's were on the rise. Mr. Harper and his colleagues were anxious to govern, even though they faced a very uncertain situation in the House of Commons. In politics, the momentum of the day can be compelling. And so Mr. Harper formed the twelfth minority government in Canadian history at the federal level.

Though keen to accept the Governor General's commission to form a government, Mr. Harper has not been a happy minority government prime minister. He has made it clear, time and time again, that he would like—and that he needs—a majority government. In this he is no different from all who have been or who aspire to be prime minister. From the prime minister's perspective, it is much easier to govern if your party has a majority in the House of Commons.

As a matter of fact, if you or I were faced with the prospect of being prime minister, we would probably prefer to lead a majority rather than a minority government, too; it really *is* much easier to govern when your party has a majority in the House. A majority government can stay totally "on message"— even if that message has been rejected at the polls by a majority of voters. There is no need to make any concessions to opposing points of view. A majority government will not have to bother with tiresome parliamentary debates or parliamentary committees it cannot control. From the perspective of prime ministers, majority government is clearly the preferred option.

But I do not think majority governments are so good for *you*, dear reader, unless—and this is a big unless—you do not want to be governed by a parliamentary government. If you prefer prime-ministerial, CEO-style government—governing without meaningful parliamentary debate and regardless of popular support in the country—then go for it. Use your vote to give the leader of one of the larger parties control of government for four years. But I hope that, like me, you prefer parliamentary government, and will vote for the party or candidate of your choice, without worrying about whether any party will have a majority.

My main aim in what follows is to explain why a minority government is not only the most likely outcome of the next election, but—contrary to what you may hear from Mr. Harper or other party leaders—is also, for most of us, the best possible outcome. Minority governments have their problems, and I will address them later in this book; note that I am giving minority government only two "cheers." I find it difficult to muster even one cheer for its main alternative—false majority government.

In the end, even if I fail to convince you of the merits of minority government, I hope that this book will help both you and our politicians make the most of minority government, give it more stability, and make it work as well as it can for our country. For, whether you like it or not, we are going to have a lot of minority government in the future. So let's make it work as well as possible—and learn to enjoy it rather than curse it.

CHAPTER TWO

Alternatives

Parliamentary elections can result in four types of government. To assess the merits of minority government, it is essential to consider the alternatives.

Two of these are based on parliaments in which one party has a majority of seats in the elected chamber. The first of these is what I call a true majority government. This is a government by leaders of a political party that has won both a majority of seats in the House of Commons and a majority of the popular vote. A true majority government has, in effect, a double majority—it is favoured by a majority of the electorate as well as by a majority of the members in the assembly the election has produced.

The second kind of majority government is led by a party that has won a majority of seats in the House of Commons but has obtained less than 50% of the popular vote. I call such governments "false" majority governments because their leaders, once in power, have a tendency to act as if they have a popular mandate from the people when in fact they do not. The media often speak in these terms, strengthening the illusion. False majority governments can only happen because our current electoral system does not reward parties with seats in numbers proportional to their share of the popular vote.

As an aside, my main purpose in writing this book is *not* to make the case for changing our first-past-the-post, simple plurality electoral system to one that produces parliaments more reflective of voter preferences. I happen to favour such reform, and hope that its time will soon come. If and when it does, it will eliminate false majority governments, but until then false majority governments will remain the most common alternative to minority governments. My aim, therefore, is to convince you that it is better to be governed by a minority government than by its most likely alternative—a false majority government. I also hope that this book will serve to counter those who argue against electoral reform on the grounds that proportional representation (an alternative electoral system in which parties gain seats in proportion to the number of votes cast for them) will make minority government virtually inevitable. The defenders of the electoral status quo would have you believe that minority government is something we should strive to avoid. It is my contention that they are wrong. Compared with false majority government, minority government is good for parliamentary democracy and good for you if, as I do, you want to be governed by parliamentary government.

The two remaining possible types of government are based on parliaments in which no party has a majority in the House of Commons. In the first type, called coalition government, cabinet positions are filled by members of two or more parties. Coalitions are usually formed when a large party that has a plurality in the legislature but not a majority offers cabinet positions to members of one or more smaller parties whose support will give the coalition government an overall majority. The other type of government is a minority government formed by a party that lacks a majority in the elected legislature but is able to stay in power by maintaining the confidence of the House of Commons. A minority government does this not by including members of other parties in the cabinet, but by winning support for its program from enough opposition members in the House to avoid defeat on measures of importance to it.

Coalition governments, although common elsewhere in the parliamentary world, are very rare in Canada, for reasons I will discuss. In our country, minority governments are the most likely type of government to result from an election that produces what is called a "hung parliament"—a parliament in which no party has a majority in the elected chamber. This means that, today, the alternative kinds of government that we as Canadians can expect when we go to the polls basically boil down to two: a false majority government or a minority government. To appreciate this point, it helps to look briefly at how our parliamentary system has performed over time.

The Historical Record

Since Confederation, Canadians have participated in 39 federal general elections and created 39 Parliaments. Table 1 lists these Parliaments and the governments they have produced.[1]

TABLE 1   CANADA'S GOVERNMENTS: 1867–2006

Parliaments	Governments	Seats in House of Commons	% of seats	% of popular vote	Type
1st 1867–72	Macdonald (Cons.)	108	60	50	TM
2nd 1872–4	Macdonald (Cons.)	104	52	50	TM
3rd 1874–8	Mackenzie (Lib.)	138	67	54	TM
4th 1878–82	Macdonald (Cons.)	142	69	53	TM
5th 1882	Macdonald (Cons.)	139	67	51	TM
6th 1887	Macdonald (Cons.)	126	59	50	TM
7th 1891	Macdonald/Abbott/ Thompson/Bowell/ Tupper (Cons.)	121	56	51	TM
8th 1896	Laurier (Lib.)	118	55	45	FM
9th 1900	Laurier (Lib.)	133	62	51	TM
10th 1904	Laurier (Lib.)	138	65	52	TM
11th 1908	Laurier (Lib.)	135	61	50	TM
12th 1911	Borden (Cons.)	134	61	51	TM
13th 1917	Borden/Meighen (Unionist)	153	65	57	COAL
14th 1921	King (Lib.)	116	49	41	MIN
15th 1925	King (Lib.)	99	40	40	MIN
1926	Meighen (Cons.)	116	47	47	MIN
16th 1926	King (Lib.)	117	48	46	MIN
17th 1930	Bennett (Cons.)	137	56	49	FM
18th 1935	King (Lib.)	173	71	45	FM
19th 1940	King (Lib.)	181	74	52	TM
20th 1945	King/St. Laurent (Lib.)	125	51	41	FM
21st 1949	St. Laurent (Lib.)	193	74	49	FM
22nd 1953	St. Laurent (Lib.)	171	65	49	FM

23rd 1957	Diefenbaker (Cons.)	105	40	39	MIN
24th 1958	Diefenbaker (Cons.)	208	79	54	TM
25th 1962	Diefenbaker (Cons.)	116	44	37	MIN
26th 1963	Pearson (Lib.)	129	49	42	MIN
27th 1965	Pearson/Trudeau (Lib.)	131	49	40	MIN
28th 1968	Trudeau (Lib.)	155	59	46	FM
29th 1972	Trudeau (Lib.)	109	41	38	MIN
30th 1974	Trudeau (Lib.)	141	53	43	FM
31st 1979	Clark (Cons.)	136	48	36	MIN
32nd 1980	Trudeau/Turner (Lib.)	147	52	44	FM
33rd 1984	Mulroney (Cons.)	211	75	50	TM
34th 1988	Mulroney/Campbell (Cons.)	169	57	43	FM
35th 1993	Chrétien (Lib.)	177	60	41	FM
36th 1997	Chrétien (Lib.)	155	51	39	FM
37th 2000	Chrétien/Martin (Lib.)	172	57	41	FM
38th 2004	Martin (Lib.)	135	44	37	MIN
39th 2006	Harper (Cons.)	124	40	36	MIN

In all but one of these Parliaments, although prime ministers have changed, there has been no change in the party controlling government throughout the life of the Parliament. The one exception is the 15th Parliament, elected in October 1925. That, of course, was the Parliament that experienced the famous King–Byng crisis when, in June 1926, Governor General Byng refused the dissolution of Parliament requested by Liberal Prime Minister Mackenzie King and called on Arthur Meighen, the Conservative leader whose party had more seats than the Liberals (though not a majority), to form a government. A few days later, Meighen's government was defeated in the House but carried on through the summer as a caretaker government until the election of September 1926. Thus, although we have had 39 Parliaments, we have had 40 governments.

Next to each government and its prime ministers, Table 1 shows first the number of seats and then the percentage of seats of each government in the House of Commons. Finally, it shows the governing party's percentage of the popular vote in each election and the type of government that resulted. TM stands for true majority government (those that had 50% or more of the seats and 50% or more of the votes); FM stands for false majority government (those that had over 50% of the seats but less than 50% of the popular vote); COAL refers to the one and only coalition government Canada has had at the federal level; and MIN indicates minority government (those that had less than 50% of the seats and less than 50% of the popular vote).

Table 2 summarizes the information in Table 1. It divides our parliamentary history into two periods—the first from 1867 to 1917, covering the first 13 federal elections, and the second covering the 26 elections we have had since 1921. What jumps out of this table is the stark contrast between the two

TABLE 2   TYPES OF GOVERNMENT SINCE 1867

	1867–1917	1921–2006	TOTAL
True Majority	11	3	14
False Majority	1	12	13
Coalition	1	0	1
Minority	0	12	12
TOTAL	13	27	40

periods. In Canada's first half-century, true majority governments were the norm; all but two of the first thirteen elections
resulted in true majority governments. Since then, however,
true majorities have been a rare election result. In only 3 of the
26 federal elections we have had since 1921 has a party managed to win a majority of the popular vote. Mackenzie King's
Liberals did it in the wartime election of 1940. In John Diefenbaker's 1958 landslide win, the Progressive Conservatives won
54% of the popular vote, equalling the all-time record set by
Alexander Mackenzie's Liberals in the Pacific Scandal election
of 1874. Brian Mulroney's Progressive Conservatives were the
last party to win a majority of the popular vote, which they did
by finishing just over the 50% mark in the 1984 election.

The Emergence of Multi-party Democracy

The reason for this sharp change in election results and types
of government is clear: it is the result of moving from a two-
party system to a multi-party system. Elections in Canada's
early days were contests between Conservatives and Liberals –
Tory *bleus* versus Liberal *rouges*, "tweedledum" versus "twee-
dledee." Voters had just two parties to choose from, and the
one that a majority voted for would form the government.

The only exceptions were the 1896 and 1917 elections. In the
1896 election, followers of D'Alton McCarthy who thought
Charles Tupper's Conservatives were too soft in permitting
French-language education in English Canada broke away from
the Conservatives and contested nine ridings. A new farmers'
organization, the Patrons of Industry, also ran candidates in 26
ridings. These two political groups outside the main two parties
were able to garner 9% of the popular vote. As a result, the

Laurier Liberals were able to win a majority of seats in the House of Commons with only 45% of the popular vote—one percentage point less than the Conservatives.

The other exception occurred in the very last election in this early period, the 1917 election that returned Robert Borden's Unionists to power. The Borden Unionist government was the only coalition government we have had at the federal level in Canada. It was formed before the 1917 election when the Laurier Liberals split over the issue of conscription and a group of pro-conscription Liberals from western Canada joined the Borden government. In the 1917 election, with few exceptions, Conservatives and Liberal conscriptionists did not run against each other. The result was a landslide win for the Borden government in the most divisive election in Canadian history. Unionists swept Ontario and the West and did well in the Maritimes, while the Liberals took all but 3 of Quebec's 65 seats.[2]

The Unionist coalition government did not last long. In 1919, when the government refused to reduce tariffs, T.A. Crerar resigned from the cabinet and nine western Unionists withdrew their support for the government. That same year, Wilfrid Laurier died and the Liberals held Canada's first national political convention, choosing Mackenzie King as their new leader. Under King's leadership, the Liberals were able to make some progress in recovering support outside of Quebec. In the 1921 election, the Liberals won the most seats but did not win a majority, and King formed Canada's first minority government. But the real news was that the Conservatives, now led by Arthur Meighen, came third. A new political party, the Progressives, led by Crerar, came second, sweeping the western provinces and taking 24 seats in Ontario. Canada had entered a new era of politics.

From the 1920s on, Canadian politics has been a contest between three or more political parties. Conservatives (in various
guises) and Liberals have usually been the strongest parties, and
only the Conservatives and Liberals have formed governments.
But throughout our modern history, the two so-called "old-line"
parties have had to compete with one or more other parties.
From the 1920s to the mid-1930s, when the Progressives were
fading away and the Co-operative Commonwealth Federation
(or CCF) and Social Credit parties had not yet emerged, the
challenge presented by so-called "third parties" was relatively
slight. Even then, however, the challenge facing the Liberals and
Conservatives was strong enough to deny Mackenzie King a
majority government in the 1920s and both King and R.B. Bennett, the Conservative leader, popular majorities in the 1930s.

Since 1935, except for the three elections that produced true
majority governments, "third parties" have garnered 20% or
more of the popular vote. Of course, unless these third parties,
like the Bloc Québécois, focus all their efforts in one region of
the country, the first-past-the-post electoral system does not reward them with House of Commons seats proportional to their
strength in the country. Still, these "third parties" do well enough
in most elections to deny the larger parties popular majorities.
As a result, 24 of the 26 federal elections held since 1921 have
produced either minority governments or false majority governments. The reason for this is simple: Canadian electorates have
ceased to be divided along a single Liberal/Conservative fault
line and are instead divided in more than two ways. Indeed, if
our Parliaments reflected the political preferences of the people,
all but three of the elections we have had since 1921 would
have resulted in minority or coalition governments.

Despite the fact that we have had a dozen of them by now, hung parliaments and minority governments are still widely regarded in Canada as aberrant deviations from the norm. So let's now take a brief look at this "deviant dozen"—their strengths and their weaknesses, their failures and their achievements.

Notes

1. My principal sources for these data are the *Canadian Parliamentary Guide*; J. Murray Beck, *Pendulum of Power: Canada's Federal Elections* (Toronto: Prentice Hall, 1968); and the Politics Canada website, www.canadawebpages.com/pc-electStats.asp.

2. The Unionist government was not the kind of coalition that results when a large party shares government with a smaller party in order to have a majority in Parliament. It was much more like the coalition government Winston Churchill's Conservatives formed with the Labour Party and the Liberals in the Second World War.

CHAPTER THREE

Minority Governments by the Dozen

At the federal level Canada has had twelve minority governments, all of them since 1921. Aside from their tendency to be short lived, these governments have had little in common. Each has been shaped by the political dynamics of its time, and each bears the stamp of its prime minister's personality. Some have accomplished a lot, and some very little. Consideration of how these twelve minority governments have performed will help us appreciate the circumstances and the kind of political leadership that maximize the potential benefits of governing without a parliamentary majority, as well as the conditions and leadership style that produce frustration and failure in minority government circumstances.

Four in the Twenties and the King–Byng Crisis

The first four minority governments were all in the 1920s—three led by Mackenzie King and one by Arthur Meighen. King's first—and Canada's first—was a classic instance of the largest party in the House enjoying the steady and sufficient support of an ideologically friendly smaller party. That is a recipe for minority government stability, and it surely was for Mackenzie King, whose 116 Liberals, combined with 64 Progressives, enjoyed four years of easy sailing in a 235-member House. Many of the Progressive MPs were former Liberals, and when two of them crossed the floor to join the Liberals in 1922, King temporarily had a majority in the House. But when the Liberals lost two by-elections in 1923, King's government was back in a minority position. King tried to lure leading Progressives, including Crerar, their leader, into his cabinet—not as members of a coalition government, but as Liberals. The Progressives balked at this, as they wished to retain their identity as a separate movement of agrarian protest. They agreed to support the King government so long as its legislative program was progressive—which in those days meant, essentially, anti-tariff.

If King had offered coalition, the Progressive leadership would likely have accepted it. But because the Liberals were anxious to unify their party, whose split led to the Unionist coalition in 1917, coalition was not offered.[1] In modern Canadian politics, this is as close as we have come to a coalition government. This first minority government set the pattern for the future: hung parliaments would result not in multi-party coalition governments, but in minority governments sustained by parliamentary alliances.

Though parliamentary conditions were propitious for legislative collaboration between Liberals and Progressives, this first minority government attempted—and achieved—very little. This was not because it was a minority government, but because

Mackenzie King was a very cautious politician, preoccupied with holding together the Montreal-based big business and Western reform wings of his party. King's first minority government, like his last, lived the course of a normal parliamentary life without fear of defeat. It ended in the autumn of 1925, when King asked the Governor General to dissolve Parliament and call an election. Although King's first government attempted and achieved very little in domestic policy, King took a strong stand in asserting Canada's independence from Great Britain in foreign policy, setting the stage for the recognition of Dominion autonomy in 1926.

King's second minority government was anything but clear sailing. His Liberals came out of the October 29, 1925 election with 99 seats—17 fewer than the 116 garnered by Meighen's Conservatives. The Progressives, whose 24 members could give either party a majority in the 245-member House through their support, held the balance of power, while 3 Labour representatives and 3 Independents held the remaining 6 seats. Immediately after the election, Prime Minister King considered resigning. When he met with Governor General Byng the following day, Byng suggested that the "dignified" course for King to take would be to resign and have the Governor General invite Meighen to form a government. But after a weekend of reflection, King decided to carry on and meet the new Parliament. In his diary, he wrote: "The argument I have felt most is the right of the people to govern themselves, by whoever [sic] their representatives decide."[2]

King faced a formidable challenge in preparing for the new Parliament that would finally assemble on January 7, 1926. Although he had lost his own seat and eight of his ministers had been defeated, King would not reconstruct his cabinet or look for a seat for himself. Portfolios would be assigned on a temporary basis to elected members. King made a point of insisting that it would be the Parliament that the people had chosen that would decide who was to govern. He crafted a Speech from the Throne (the speech prepared by the government and read by the Governor General that opens a new session of Parliament by setting out the government's plans for the session) that the Progressives and Labour MPs were prepared to support. King's efforts were successful: on January 15, his government received enough support from the Progressives and Labour MPs to survive Meighen's amendment to the throne speech by three votes. But instead of forcing a vote on the speech itself, Meighen spun out the debate on the throne speech until March 2, when closure was used to force a vote; the speech passed with a majority of nine. Mackenzie King was as crafty a parliamentary manager as ever held prime-ministerial office. Looking back on these events today, one cannot help wondering whether these parliamentary skills would be equally successful in the age of television.

As a minority government prime minister, King again preferred a legislative alliance to the coalition government urged on him by the Progressive leader, Robert Forke. The program that resulted from this alliance contained an array of proposals designed to appeal to Progressives and Labourites, as well as to the reform wing of King's own party: for the Progressives, a commitment to increase immigration, land settlement, and railway building, and transfer control of natural resources to the western provinces; for Labour, a plan for a Canada-wide old-age pension plan. All of this was congenial to the majority in the

Liberal caucus. Progressive and Labour MPs were invited to participate in the drafting of legislation. King's earlier career as an industrial relations conciliator had prepared him well for this kind of cross-bench collaboration. His second minority government might have lasted as long as his first had it not been brought crashing down by that killer of governments—scandal.

A smelly scandal had been brewing since March 1926, when a special parliamentary committee was established to investigate allegations that officials in the Department of Customs and Excise were involved in massive smuggling through the port of Montreal. Like the sponsorship scandal in Canada's recent political history, the allegations and rumours concerned Quebec members of a federal Liberal administration. When the chairman of the committee reported to the House on Tuesday, June 22, H.H. Stevens of the Conservatives moved an amendment condemning the government's administration of the department as "wholly indefensible."[3] If this amendment carried, it would amount to a vote of non-confidence in the government.

For four feverish days and nights the House debated the Stevens amendment. Mackenzie King resorted to every parliamentary manoeuvre in the book to win enough Progressive votes for his government's survival. Late on Friday, June 25, King managed to have the debate adjourned for the weekend without the crucial vote being taken. On Saturday morning, the prime minister went to see Governor General Byng and asked him to dissolve Parliament and call an election. Byng had thought all along that Meighen—who, remember, had more seats than King—should, if he wished, have a chance to form a government, so Byng refused King's request. King called on the Governor General again at noon on Monday, June 28. When Byng once again refused his request, King submitted his resignation. In the afternoon, King told a startled House of Commons that he was no longer prime minister and then moved that the House adjourn. To King's surprise and chagrin, Meighen agreed to form a government.

And so endeth our second minority government and beginneth our third. Arthur Meighen's minority government did not last long. In forming a government, Meighen faced a challenging technicality that no longer applies to our system of parliamentary government.[4] According to the law at that time, a Member of Parliament accepting salaried office as a minister with portfolio had to resign his seat and seek re-election in a by-election. This meant that Meighen himself, in accepting the position of prime minister, had to resign his seat. As a temporary expedient, his government would be made up of unsalaried ministers without portfolio. What a set-up this was for Mackenzie King! After a day debating the customs scandal that resulted in a vote of censure on his former government, King went on the attack. For two days he launched a barrage of constitutional rhetoric at the shaky structure of the Meighen government, with Meighen not present in the House to defend its legality. Finally, at 2 a.m. on the morning of July 2, King had rattled enough Progressives to carry by a single vote a motion asserting that the ministers of the Meighen government had no right to sit in the House. The deciding vote was cast by a dozing Progressive, who, roused by the furor in the House, suddenly woke up and voted against the Meighen government, breaking an agreement not to vote (a parliamentary "pair") with a pro-government member.[5] Meighen accepted this defeat as a vote of non-confidence.

Now it was Meighen's turn to visit the Governor General and ask for a dissolution. By this time it was clear that no party could form a government that had the confidence of this Parliament. So Byng granted Prime Minister Meighen what he had denied Prime Minister King. Meighen would remain as prime minister, heading a caretaker government that would carry out the routine responsibilities of governing until an election could be held in the fall.

The King–Byng crisis of 1926 is a mythic event in Canadian history, right up there with driving the last spike in the Canadian Pacific Railway and Canada's 1972 win over Russia in hockey. Although nothing like it has occurred again in our parliamentary history, Governors General, prime ministers, and prime ministers in waiting have all been spooked by it and the lessons it might have for them. It concerns the part of our constitution that takes the form of unwritten constitutional conventions. This part of our constitutional system is not taught in law schools or, with rare exceptions, in political science courses. Nor do the passing packs of journalists assigned to cover post-election scenarios have a clue about these things. So, as an old-school political scientist brought up on debates over King–Byng, let me offer a few words about what we might take from this event.

In assessing Byng's refusal of King's request for a dissolution of Parliament, it is essential to understand the principle that must govern such a decision. The Governor General's objective must be to ensure that the Parliament the people have created has a chance to operate. In this democratic age, the head of state or her representative should act on his or her own judgment and reject a prime minister's advice only when doing so is necessary to protect parliamentary democracy. Many years ago,

Eugene Forsey, the doyen of constitutional scholars, pointed out that if a Governor General was always bound to accede to a prime minister's request for a dissolution, a government could "play a game of constitutional ping-pong in which, rejected by the electors, it appeals to the House, rejected by the House, it appeals to the electorate again, and so on indefinitely."[6] So the key question is whether Byng faced a situation in which he had to say "no" to a prime minister in order to give a newly elected Parliament a chance to function.

Two points count in Byng's favour. One is that this 15th Canadian Parliament was just eight months old; it had been sitting for only six months. It was reasonable for the Governor General to consider whether it was necessary to plunge the country into another election so soon after the last one. The second point is that a vote to censure the King government was imminent, so that granting King's request would deny the Parliament the people had elected a chance to pass judgment on his government. Even so, the Governor General would have had no choice but to grant King a dissolution had there been no apparent alternative government capable of commanding the confidence of Parliament. Byng believed that Meighen could form such a government. It turned out that he was wrong, but the question is: could Governor General Byng reasonably have been expected to foresee the quick defeat of the Meighen government?

Byng knew (or should have known), and members of Parliament knew, about the difficulty Meighen would have in forming a regular cabinet of ministers with portfolios. However, when Byng met with Robert Forke, the Progressives' leader, Forke had a written memorandum stating that the Progressive group had passed a motion "That we assist the new administration in completing the business of the session."[7] Should Byng have foreseen that the Progressives would split when exposed to King's withering attack on the legitimacy of the Meighen government, or that a slumbering Progressive MP would wake up, break a parliamentary pair, and give King the one vote he needed to defeat the Meighen government?

It is not easy to conclude that Byng was clearly wrong to have thought that Meighen's government had a chance of surviving. I find it much easier to conclude that by suddenly resigning and leaving the Governor General in the lurch without a government and with little time to explore the viability of a Meighen government, Mackenzie King used high-pressure tactics and acted dishonourably. King hoped that the Governor General, under pressure, would reconsider exploring the possibility of a Meighen government and grant King his dissolution. But Byng—who always thought that Meighen, leader of the party with the most seats in the House of Commons, should have a crack at forming a government—did not buckle. The Crown must always be advised by ministers. In commissioning Meighen to form a government, Byng resorted to the only available alternative under the circumstances.

Later in this book, I will consider what we might learn from other parliamentary democracies about how to handle the kind of situation that arose in the King–Byng affair. But even if better practices can be instituted to guide the parliamentary head of state (be it a monarchical or republican model) in determining whether all the possibilities of forming an effective government have been exhausted and that a hung parliament must be dissolved, some element of discretion will remain and the system's smooth functioning will depend on the good judgment and honourable behaviour of the key actors. That is the most fundamental lesson of the King–Byng affair.

Mackenzie King's Liberals won the 1926 election, and this is sometimes cited as evidence that the Canadian people upheld King's view that the Governor General—not King—had acted unconstitutionally in the June crisis. Certainly, King pounded away at the constitutional issue in the election campaign; it was a welcome diversion from the stench of the customs scandal. But the Liberals hardly scored a resounding victory. The Conservatives' popular vote increased by 9,000 over its vote in the 1925 election and was just 0.8% behind the Liberals'. But the Liberals elected 117 members and the Conservatives only 91. This was the first election that so prominently advertised the distorting effects of the first-past-the-post electoral system. Although the Conservatives won a third of the vote in Quebec and the Prairie provinces, they elected only four members from Quebec and one from the Prairies.

In 1926, Mackenzie King formed what was technically Canada's fourth minority government, but this was a minority government only in a formal, technical sense. Eleven members were elected as Liberal-Progressives, and King could count on them to support his government. Their numbers, plus twenty Progressives, three Labour, and three Independents—all of whom would usually support the Liberals—meant that King could manage this government as if he had a majority. This minority government lived out a normal parliamentary lifespan of four years. Among its accomplishments were two of the initiatives negotiated and launched by the previous minority government: Canada's first old-age pension scheme and a constitutional amendment giving the western provinces control over their natural resources.

Dief's Up and Down

Our next two minority governments were all about John George Diefenbaker: one on his way "up" and the other on his way "down."

The first Diefenbaker government was a huge surprise. When Canadians went to the polls on June 10, 1957, Louis St. Laurent's Liberals were expected to win. In the pipeline debate that raged on through the months leading up to the election, the Liberals had been hammered for their arrogance and contempt of Parliament. Although battered and bloodied and under relentless attack by the Conservatives' new leader, John Diefenbaker, the Liberals were still six points ahead in a poll taken two days before the election. In his wonderful chronicle of the Diefenbaker years, Peter Newman tells us that as the country went to bed waiting for the final returns, *Maclean's* was rolling out its post-election issue with an editorial stating: "For better or worse, we Canadians have once more elected one of the most powerful governments ever created by the free will of an electorate."[8] But *Maclean's*, and most everyone else, was wrong. In the election the following day, John Diefenbaker ended 22 years of Liberal rule.

The Parliament created by Canada's 23rd general election was a very hung parliament indeed. Diefenbaker's Progressive Conservatives, with 112 seats, had a plurality, while the Liberals elected 105 MPs, the CCF (precursor of the NDP) 25, and Social Credit 19 (all from the West); 4 Independents completed the 265-member House. In this situation, the Liberals had the option of hanging on and testing their strength in the new Parliament. But although the Liberals had won 2% more of the popular vote than the Tories (40.9% versus 38.9%) and the St. Laurent cabinet met two days after the election to consider its options, it quickly concluded that to hang on would be "virtual political suicide."[9] In politics, momentum is so often decisive, and at this point in Canadian politics all the momentum was with John Diefenbaker. Still, St. Laurent waited for a week, until the military vote was in, before submitting his resignation. Diefenbaker and the new Progressive Conservative government were sworn in on June 21, 1957.

This, our fifth minority government—though it lasted only nine months—was a whirlwind of activity and accomplishment. Diefenbaker radiated a sense of urgency and action. In Peter Newman's words, "The Conservatives swamped the surviving Liberals with the momentum of their legislative drive."[10] Increases in old-age pensions, unemployment insurance benefits, and National Housing Act loans; tax cuts for low income earners and small businesses; a new winter works program to combat seasonal unemployment; setting up a Royal Commission on Energy and another on Price Spreads; and a federal–provincial conference on health insurance—these were all among the measures launched in this flurry of activity. Though in a minority position, Diefenbaker showed no concern about the possibility of defeat in the House. It was clear that none of the opposition parties were in a hurry to have another election, least of all the defeated and demoralized Liberals, who were preoccupied with finding a new leader. This minority government's life was entirely in its own hands.

In the fall of 1957, word began to spread that the Diefenbaker government was on such a roll that it was considering asking for a dissolution and an election in order to take advantage of its gathering strength and win a majority. Constitutionally, can a government call for an election in the early days of a new Parliament just to cash in on a rise in its political fortunes? Eugene Forsey answered that question with an unequivocal "no." In a letter sent to Diefenbaker in late October, Forsey made the point in his usual forceful manner:[11]

> To announce, eight or ten months in advance, that whatever Parliament does, it will be dissolved next spring seems to me to be a very odd way of showing respect for Parliament. Elections are serious matters. They disrupt business. They interrupt the orderly conduct of foreign policy. They cost money, millions to the public treasury, millions more to the parties and the candidates. A second election within a year can be justified only on grounds of public necessity. A clear majority for the Government over all parties is a convenience for the Government. It is not, in itself, a public necessity. It becomes so only if the conduct of the opposition parties makes it so ... But until it does, a party committed to restoring and maintaining the rights of Parliament should allow Parliament to do the public business it was elected to do.

Diefenbaker replied to Forsey, saying that he fully agreed, but as Denis Smith, Diefenbaker's biographer, observes, "The temptation to dissolve early remained strong."[12]

In January 1958, that temptation became irresistible when Lester Pearson, making his parliamentary debut as the new Liberal leader, made a terrible mistake. In a debate on interim supply, instead of moving an amendment that would amount to a vote of non-confidence, Pearson called on the Diefenbaker government to resign and let the Liberals resume their rightful place in charge of the Government of Canada. For Diefenbaker, Pearson's motion was like raw meat waved at a hungry hound dog. He ravaged the arrogant Liberals and their new leader. Things got so bad that a kindly member of the CCF rose in the House to ask "if the Prime Minister believes in the humane slaughter of animals."[13] Ten days later, Diefenbaker flew to Quebec City to ask Governor General Vincent Massey, who was in residence at the Château Frontenac to open Quebec's Winter Carnival, to dissolve Parliament. Massey—a lifelong Liberal—agreed. Diefenbaker returned to Ottawa the same day and, with the opposition caught completely off guard, announced that there would be an election on March 31 "because the government needed a majority to protect itself from Liberal obstruction."[14]

The 1958 election resulted in the greatest landslide win in Canadian political history. The Diefenbaker Conservatives took 53.6% of the popular vote and 78.5% of the seats in the House of Commons. Alexander Mackenzie's Liberals had equalled that share of the popular vote in 1874, but the Conservatives' 208 seats gave them a position of dominance in the House of Commons unequalled by any party before or since. The Liberals were reduced to 49 seats, the CCF to 8, and the Socreds (Social Credit) were wiped out. The Tories' breakthrough in Quebec—an increase from 9 seats to 50—was extraordinary.

With this kind of electoral support and parliamentary strength, the Diefenbaker government should have been a roaring success.

It was anything but. There were difficult economic circumstances to deal with, tough foreign policy decisions to make with respect to Canada's cooperating with the United States in the nuclear defence of North America, and, with the dawning of Quebec's Quiet Revolution, more than the usual problems with managing federal–provincial relations. But over and above all of these problems was the difficult personality of John Diefenbaker. The barnstorming oratory that had brought "Dief" to power is not what is needed to direct the government of a large modern state. Diefenbaker's deficiencies and personality flaws soon became evident to his colleagues, to the media, and therefore to the public. When the writ was dropped for the federal election in the spring of 1962, Canada's love affair with John Diefenbaker was over.

In the June 1962 election, the Conservatives took a terrible beating but managed to hang on to enough seats to form our sixth minority government. In the new Parliament, the Conservatives had 116 seats (a loss of 92, including 36 of their Quebec seats) to the Liberals' 100, while the newly formed NDP (successor to the CCF) had 19. The remaining 30 seats were won by Social Credit, 26 of them in Quebec. This was the big surprise of the 1962 election. The leader of the Quebec Socreds was Réal Caouette, whose Ralliement des Créditistes de Quebec functioned as a separate Quebec party of rural protest. For the first time in federal elections, a "third party" had captured a substantial share of Quebec seats—a harbinger, as we now know, of things to come.

Diefenbaker's second minority government was the polar opposite of his first. This one was sour and destructive; very much a government run by a leader on the way down and a party deeply divided over its leader. It was mercifully put out of its misery in a few months' time. The issue that exposed Diefenbaker's weaknesses above all others was his inability to decide whether to allow nuclear warheads to be used by the missiles and aircraft his government had purchased, and that were designed for nuclear warfare. In February 1963, when a group of dissident cabinet ministers revolted against Diefenbaker, Lester Pearson seized the day and moved a vote of non-confidence in the government that, with the support of the NDP and Social Credit, carried 142 to 111. "For the second time in the century, a vote in the House had brought down a government."[15]

Two for Pearson Back to Back

The fact that Lester "Mike" Pearson led two minority governments, back to back, was hugely disappointing to Pearson and the Liberal Party. The Liberals brought about the elections that produced these minority governments in order to obtain the majority government they believed they needed and deserved. The Pearson years were rocked by scandals, by the emergence of a secular, nationalist Quebec challenging the Canadian federation, and by a raucous Parliament. The title of Peter Newman's book, *The Distemper of Our Times*,[16] captures the sour, troubled mood of these years. And yet, despite all that, this was a period of major national accomplishments. The foundations of the Canadian welfare state were completed with the adoption of the Canada Pension Plan and a national medicare program, the country finally got its own flag, the Royal Commission on Bilingualism and Biculturalism was established, and Canada celebrated its first century in style with Expo '67. Minority government years may keep us on the edge of our seats—holding our noses as we watch the political shenanigans—but that doesn't mean that nothing is accomplished.

For the Pearson Liberals, the outcome of the April 1963 election was surely a case of "snatching defeat from the jaws of victory."[17] Going into the election, the Liberals had all the momentum—a successful policy conference, a clutch of new talent, and a Nobel Peace Prize winner as leader running against a bloodied and humiliated John Diefenbaker. Yet with so much going for them, they obtained only 41.7% of the popular vote and their 129 seats fell 4 short of a majority in the House. Diefenbaker, with 95 Conservative seats and 32.8% of the popular vote, was beaten—but not as badly as the Liberals had hoped. The NDP with 17 members and the Socreds with 24 (20 from Quebec), and 25% of the popular vote between them, showed how hard it had become to win a majority mandate in Canada's multi-party system.

In his memoirs, Mike Pearson tells us that he "was not really worried about a defeat in the House during the two years after 1963."[18] Pearson didn't have to worry, because the Liberals at this time were clearly left-leaning and could count on the NDP to support their program. His real problems were Diefenbaker and Quebec. It was Dief's ability in opposition to take advantage of the Liberals' troubles with scandal and with Quebec, and the anxiety of finding a way of placating Quebec without weakening Canada, that wore Pearson down and made him believe that everything would be so much easier if he had a parliamentary majority. After a good deal of dithering in the summer of 1965, Pearson polled his cabinet. With the majority favouring an early election, on September 7, Pearson asked the Governor General to dissolve Parliament for a November 8 election.

With two and a half years elapsed since the last election, no question was raised about the constitutionality of calling for an election without a defeat in the House. But the results of the 1965 election call into question the necessity of such an early dissolution. The 1965 election goes down in history as the election that marked the least change in the electorate's preferences. The Liberals did not win the parliamentary majority they so dearly coveted, nor did they slay John Diefenbaker. The Liberals and Conservatives each gained two seats. The Liberals' popular vote actually dropped a point and a half, while the Conservatives' went up by four and a half. The NDP picked up four more seats with an increase of just under 5% in its popular vote. The main losers were the Socreds, who, during the campaign, split into two separate parties–Robert Thompson's Alberta rump taking five seats and Caouette's Créditistes nine.

In terms of scandal, partisan rancour, and the strains of Quebec nationalism on the federation, Pearson's second minority government was a replay of his first. And though again it was productive—implementing medicare, establishing a new system of fiscal federalism, and dispatching France's President Charles de Gaulle after his "Vive le Québec libre" speech in Montreal—the stress (which would have been just as great had he won a majority) wore Pearson down. Canadians had grown tired of watching a worn-out Pearson and a burnt-out Diefenbaker duking it out. They wanted new national leaders, and they got them. In September 1967, the Conservatives elected Robert Stanfield their new leader. In December 1967, Mike Pearson announced his decision to retire, and in early April 1968, the

Liberals chose Pierre Elliot Trudeau as their new leader. Trudeau wasted no time seeking a mandate from the people. Within two weeks of becoming Liberal leader and prime minister of Canada, he had Parliament dissolved for a June 25 election.

A Pretty Good but Ominous One for Trudeau

In the 1968 election, "Trudeaumania" delivered the parliamentary majority that the Liberals wanted so much to recover. Their 46% of the popular vote translated into 155 seats and a healthy majority in the House of Commons. When Trudeau called an election in September 1972, his government fully expected to keep its majority. But this time, Trudeau failed to deliver. A lackadaisical Liberal campaign with the lame slogan "The Land Is Strong," a solid campaign by Stanfield focusing on economic issues, and a punchy performance by David Lewis, the new NDP leader, attacking "corporate welfare bums" resulted in a very hung parliament. The Liberals elected 109 MPs, just 2 more than the Conservatives. The NDP elected 31 members— its best result yet—and clearly held the balance of power in the House of Commons.

Trudeau's one and only experience with minority government went pretty well. It was a classic legislative alliance between a governing party and an ideologically friendly smaller party. What made it work was a temporary change in Trudeau's leadership style and a cagey parliamentary tactician on the government side. Trudeau, in the words of Trudeau's biographers, Stephen Clarkson and Christina McCall, made a "startling switch": He softened his in-the-face, high-handed manner, stopped referring to MPs as "nobodies," became a "pragmatic politician,"[19] and had the good sense to enlist as his House Leader a veteran parliamentarian, Allan MacEachen.

It was MacEachen who managed the relationship with the NDP. Although Lewis's official position was that he refused to have an alliance with the Liberals or the Conservatives, he met on several occasions with MacEachen, without either his caucus or the Liberal cabinet knowing, to negotiate important policy issues such as the size of the pension increase and the size of the corporate tax cut in Finance Minister John Turner's budget.[20] Lewis made his demands, and the Liberals delivered on enough of them to get Trudeau's minority government through its first eighteen months without a serious threat to its survival. Part of its success in surviving was minimizing the votes that would be regarded as confidence issues.

By the summer of 1973, as Richard Gwyn has written, "Trudeau and MacEachen had reached their point of no return."[21] Enough time had gone by since the last election that, if defeated on a confidence vote, they could have a dissolution rather than giving Stanfield a chance to form a government. And so, they began to look for the opportunity of being defeated in the House. In the spring of 1974, very cleverly, they baited the hook. They concocted a budget with just enough in it to offend the NDP. Lewis took the bait, and combined with the Conservatives to defeat Turner's budget. The Trudeau minority government was the third to be terminated by an opposition vote in the House and the first to be defeated on a budget vote. Never was a government happier in defeat!

The Trudeau minority government was "pretty good" because it formed an effective legislative alliance with the NDP that accomplished a good deal, including major improvements in social security, legislation on election expenses and foreign investment, and the appointment of Justice Thomas Berger, a former leader of the NDP in British Columbia, to head the Mackenzie Valley Pipeline Inquiry. All of this, of course, had a leftward tilt, but bear in mind that the combined popular vote of the Liberals and NDP in the 1972 election was 56%. Moving Canadian policy in a social democratic direction was not out of step with the preferences of a majority of Canadians.

But the Trudeau minority government was ominous in that it was an interlude between Liberal majority governments that were becoming increasingly unparliamentary. Trudeau, the rational planner and charismatic leader, had little use for parliament as an institution. The Trudeau years witnessed a major expansion in the size of the Prime Minister's Office (PMO) and the influence on government of unelected political advisers who, unlike cabinet ministers, have no other base for their power than the prime minister's regard. Trudeau made few of his major speeches in Parliament. He preferred to be a "plebiscitary leader," communicating directly with the people rather than debating the great issues of the day in Parliament.[22] With a majority of seats in the House of Commons, he would be relieved of any need to accommodate the views of political parties representing the majority of Canadians who had voted against him and his party.

Clark's Catastrophe

Our next minority government, headed by Joe Clark, lasted less than seven months, from May 22 to December 12, 1979. Only Arthur Meighen's was shorter. Clark's minority government need not have been so short lived. Its brevity was the result of its leader's unwillingness to deal realistically with the Conservatives' minority position and the Conservative leadership's unfounded confidence in being able to score a knockout blow in an election if defeated on an early non-confidence vote.

Under their new leader, Joe Clark, the Progressive Conservatives did well in the 1979 election, although not nearly as well as they seemed to think. With 136 seats to the Liberals' 114 and the NDP's 26, the PCs had a plurality in the House of Commons. The 6 Créditistes from Quebec clearly held the balance of power. After the election, the Trudeau government felt defeated and did not hesitate to step aside and let Clark's Conservatives form a government. The Clark government's hold on power in a 282-member House depended very much on the support of the 6 Créditistes. Yet Clark and his colleagues seemed oblivious to their tenuous hold on power. Clark declined to meet with Créditiste leader Fabien Roy and negotiate the terms on which the Créditistes would support the government. Although his party had received only 36% of the popular vote—four points less than the Liberals—the day after the election Clark said: "I am proceeding on the assumption that the Progressive Conservative Party has won a mandate to govern. I intend to carry out that mandate."[23]

The nearly five months that elapsed between the May 22 election and October 9, when Canada's 31st Parliament held its first meeting, was the longest hiatus in Canadian parliamentary history. When Parliament finally did meet, the weakness of the Clark government's position quickly became apparent. It faced a steady barrage of non-confidence votes, which it managed to survive by the skin of its teeth—as much through Liberal absenteeism as Socred support. The reappointment of Liberal

James Jerome as Speaker meant one less member of the opposition and so eased the situation a bit, but this was more than offset in November when the Conservatives lost two by-elections, one to the NDP and one to the Liberals. When Conservative MP David Kilgour told Clark that the Créditistes were willing to enter into "an informal coalition" to enable the government to survive for eighteen months, Clark spurned the offer. Pierre Trudeau's announcement on November 21 that he was retiring from politics contributed to the Conservatives' overconfidence about their prospects should the government be defeated in the House and an election ensue.

And that is exactly what did happen when Finance Minister John Crosbie introduced his budget on December 11. At no time would Crosbie's budget, with its expenditure cuts and tax increases—"short-term pain for long-term gain"—be an easy sell. In the Clark government's precarious parliamentary situation, it amounted to political suicide. The Créditistes made it clear that they could not accept the 18% increase in the excise tax on gasoline. The Liberals, despite being without a leader, showed signs of being prepared to defeat the government. The Conservatives—despite the absence of 6 of their members and polling results that showed them trailing the Liberals by 17 points—instead of postponing the vote until all their members were back, allowed a vote on the budget to take place on the evening of December 13. With the Socreds abstaining, the Liberals and NDP combined to defeat the budget by a vote of 139 to 133.

The denouement of this Tory catastrophe is that five days later Pierre Trudeau announced that he had changed his mind; he was not retiring. The Liberals would not have to hold a leadership convention. Trudeau would lead the party in the election called for February 18. The Trudeau-led Liberals won that election and, with a 4% increase in their popular vote, were able to form a majority government.

A Tormented Martin Learns the Discipline of Minority Government

After the fall of the Clark minority government, Canada experienced nearly a quarter-century of majority governments at the federal level. This long period of majority government rule strengthened the tendency of Canadians to think of majority government as the norm and of minority government as a scary aberration. And it certainly did nothing to dissuade Canada's governing parties that majority government was the only acceptable election result. But the election results on which this spate of majority governments was based did not indicate that Canadian voters had strong majoritarian preferences. Only Brian Mulroney's first Progressive Conservative government in 1984 was supported by a majority of voters, and even then by just the slimmest of majorities. After that, voter support for the governing parties was never higher than 43%. The "friendly dictatorships" of the Chrétien years never garnered more than 41%.[24]

When the Liberals chose Paul Martin as their new leader on November 14, 2003, he was given "the strongest mandate of any Liberal leader in at least half a century."[25] On the first and only ballot, Martin won 3,242 out of 3,453 votes. Who would have guessed that seven months later Martin would become the first new leader of an incumbent government to lose its majority? But that's exactly what happened.

Martin's slide resulted mainly from two factors. First was the uniting of the right—the merger of the Progressive Conservatives and the Canadian Alliance, and the election of Stephen Harper (on the third ballot) as the first leader of the Conservative Party of Canada in March 2004. Prime Minister Martin would not benefit, as Jean Chrétien had, from the absence of a serious governing party alternative to the Liberals. The second factor was scandal—specifically, the scandal that followed in the wake of the Auditor General's disclosure of improprieties in the Liberal government's sponsorship program in Quebec. The aim of the program was to strengthen the federalist cause through advertising campaigns displaying symbols of Canadian government sponsorship of popular public events in Quebec. Despite (some would say because of) Martin's efforts to show he was doing the "right thing" about the scandal by appointing Justice John Gomery to conduct a public inquiry into the allegations, the smell of scandal stuck to his administration and would eventually lead to the demise of his minority government.

Canadians elected their 38th Parliament on June 28, 2004, and it was a very hung parliament indeed. The Martin Liberals, despite losing only four points of the popular vote (41% to 37%), saw their seats in the House plummet from 172 to 135. The new Conservative Party won only 30% of the popular vote, ten points less than the combined popular support for the Alliance and Progressive Conservative parties in the 2000 election. But because there was now no splitting of the conservative vote in individual ridings, the Conservative Party emerged with 99 seats in the House—19 more than the Alliance and PCs had held in the previous Parliament. The NDP made the biggest gain in popular vote, moving from 9% to 16%, but this yielded only a modest gain in seats, from 13 to 19. The biggest gain in seats was made by the Bloc Québécois. Their increase in popular vote from 11% to 12% translated into a 16-seat increase in the House of Commons, from 38 to 54.

After the election, there was no doubt that the Martin government would carry on. But its position in the new Parliament was precarious. With Liberal Peter Milliken continuing as Speaker, the Liberals and their natural legislative ally, the NDP, would have 153 seats—exactly the same number as the combined numbers of the Conservatives and Bloc Québécois. In this 308-member House, the one Independent member, former Conservative Chuck Cadman, would hold the balance of power.

As they approached their first encounter with Parliament, Prime Minister Paul Martin and his advisers showed that they had a lot to learn about the discipline of governing with a minority. Instead of following the examples of Mackenzie King and Pierre Trudeau and finding out what was needed to secure opposition support for their throne speech, Martin and his "board" of political advisers took Joe Clark's approach and prepared to meet Parliament as if the government had a majority. In September 2004, nearly a month before Parliament was due to assemble, the leaders of the three opposition parties issued a joint statement warning that they were prepared to defeat the government if the throne speech made no effort to accommodate their priorities. Harper, Bloc leader Gilles Duceppe, and NDP leader Jack Layton also wrote to Governor General Adrienne Clarkson, urging her "to consider all of your options" in the event that the Martin government was defeated in the throne speech debate and the prime minister asked for a dissolution of Parliament and a snap election.[26] The opposition leaders were noticeably silent on what option any of them were prepared to support. The game of "political chicken" had begun. For the next three years it would be a constant and troublesome feature of our national politics.

When the 38th Parliament opened on October 5, 2004, party leaders continued to play the political chicken game. The Speech from the Throne made no concessions to the opposition parties' priorities. Word was out that the Bloc and Conservatives were preparing amendments to the throne speech that, if they carried, would be regarded by many as a vote of non-confidence in the government. Sanity returned on the evening of October 7, when a chastened Prime Minister Martin cut a deal with the Bloc and the Conservatives, watering down a Bloc motion that was the first of the hostile amendments aimed at the throne speech. A motion proposing, of all things, that "financial pressures the provinces are suffering as a consequence of the fiscal imbalance be alleviated, as demanded by the Premier of Quebec" be replaced by a motion that called for the alleviation of the "financial pressures some call the fiscal imbalance."[27] Martin could accept this motion as a "friendly" amendment to the throne speech.

After this exercise in brinkmanship, the government and opposition parties cooled things down and began to operate in the way that minority government parliamentarians should. The government agreed to accommodate opposition demands enough for it to survive without abandoning essential elements of its program, and enough for opposition leaders to say they had not caved in entirely on advancing their priorities. Party officials worked out the key agreement over the weekend of October 16–17. The points that the Conservatives wanted to push in their throne speech amendments were taken care of in

a variety of ways. Their proposal to create an independent em-
ployment insurance commission would be studied by a parliamentary committee. A pre-budget consultation process would
consider tax cuts for low-income Canadians. The Commons
would hold a non-binding vote on Canada's participation in US
anti-missile defence. The NDP's proposal to have a citizens'
assembly review electoral reform would be given consideration.[28] And so on. This modus vivendi enabled the government
to carry on without a serious threat to its survival until the
spring budget debate approached.

The sponsorship scandal continued to hang over the Martin
government like a thick black cloud obliterating its positive accomplishments, such as the child-care agreements it negotiated
with the provinces and its bolstering of urban infrastructure.
In April 2005, when the Gomery Commission's public hearings
began, the clouds burst and details of fraudulent contracts and
kickbacks of dirty money to the Liberal Party rained down daily
on the government. By April 21, Prime Minister Martin felt so
much under siege that he spoke to the nation in a televised
evening broadcast, apologizing for the "unjustifiable mess" of
the sponsorship program and promising an election 30 days
after Justice Gomery's final report was delivered.[29]

Martin's commitment to have an election after the full
Gomery report was released did not satisfy Stephen Harper or
Gilles Duceppe. They smelt blood and thirsted for a chance to
defeat the government. The opposition wanted an immediate
election on the sponsorship scandal before the Martin government had a chance to shape the election agenda with a new
budget. On May 10, the Bloc and Conservatives combined forces
to pass a motion, by a vote of 153 to 150, calling for the Martin

government to resign.[30] The Liberals maintained that because this motion came on a procedural point they would not treat it as a vote of non-confidence. Martin promised that there would be an opportunity for the opposition to move non-confidence before the end of the month. At this point, the Bloc and Conservative leaders became enraged. For a week they made Parliament unworkable, boycotting committees, cancelling question period, and adjourning House business early in the day. Harper and Duceppe called for Governor General Adrienne Clarkson to intervene and persuade the Martin government to resign. They shied away from spelling out what Madam Clarkson should do if the prime minister did not follow her advice.

The Bloc and the Conservatives finally got their chance to bring down the government on Thursday, May 18, when the House would vote on two budget bills, one of which resulted from an agreement with the NDP to implement an additional $4.6 billion of social policy expenditures. The days leading up to the vote were filled with high drama. On the morning of May 16, Belinda Stronach, runner-up to Stephen Harper in the Conservative leadership vote, announced (after hours of pillow talk with her shocked and broken-hearted lover, Peter Mackay, the deputy leader of the Conservatives) that she was crossing the floor of the House and would take a portfolio in the Liberal government.[31] Chalk up one more vote for the government and one less for its parliamentary opponents. The fate of the government was now in the hands of three Independents: David Kilgour, who was pressing the government to take action to stop the genocide in the Darfur region of Sudan; Carolyn Parrish, who had been booted out of the Liberal caucus for making unkind remarks about US President George Bush; and Chuck

Cadman, who was undergoing chemotherapy treatments for cancer. In the end, the redoubtable Cadman managed to get to Ottawa to vote for the government. His vote, along with Parrish's, produced a tie: 152–152. Speaker Peter Milliken broke the tie, casting the deciding vote for the government.[32] The Martin government had survived, but only by the skin of its teeth.

After this cliffhanger, the political scene cooled down for a while. But following the summer break, it heated up again, particularly after the release of the first volume of the Gomery Inquiry report detailing all the skullduggery of the sponsorship scandal. Now the NDP, having got its $4.6 billion reward for supporting the Liberal government in the May budget vote, found the stench of the sponsorship scandal unbearable. With Justice Gomery's final report containing his policy recommendations due in early February, the election promised by the prime minister would take place sometime in March. But for NDP leader Jack Layton, that was too long to live with such a dishonourable government. On November 21, Layton's motion to call an election in early January for a mid-February vote carried 167 to 129.[33] The opposition leaders gave the Martin government one week to accept this election timing or face defeat on a non-confidence motion. The government refused to back down. On November 28, 2005, Stephen Harper's non-confidence motion, supported by the Bloc and NDP, carried easily at 171 to 133. Prime Minister Martin announced that he would ask for an immediate dissolution and the beginning of an election campaign that would extend through the Christmas holidays to a vote on January 23.[34]

Technically, Martin's government was the fifth minority government to have its life terminated by an opposition vote. But, like the other six, it would have been responsible for ending its own life had the opposition not been so impatient to have an election a few weeks earlier than promised by the government.

A Grumpy Harper Learns How to Govern with a Minority

On January 23, 2006, Canadian voters elected another hung parliament. Stephen Harper's Conservatives had done the best, winning 125 seats with 36% of the popular vote. The Liberals, with 30% of the popular vote, won 102. The Bloc elected 51 MPs, although its popular vote of 11% fell far short of the NDP's, whose 18% garnered them only 29 seats. One Quebec Independent completed the membership of the 308-member House.

The day after the election, Prime Minister Martin told the Governor General he intended to resign and advised Madam Jean to ask Harper to form a government. Harper accepted the Governor General's commission and so became the leader of Canada's twelfth minority government.

Stephen Harper had run a very focused election campaign, making it clear what his party's priorities were and what his government would do if he won the election. His government's throne speech on April 4, 2006, was short, and anchored on the five key promises in the Conservatives' election platform:

- cut the goods and services tax
- reduce hospital waiting times
- clean up the sleaze and make government more accountable
- get tougher on crime
- deliver $1,200 child-care allowances to families with young children

These five promises had become a mantra that Harper and his colleagues rattled off at every opportunity. The Speech from the Throne contained a few other pledges—notably, promises to reform the Senate, to enhance Quebec's international status, to improve relations with the United States, and to apologize to those who had paid the Chinese head tax. The Conservatives felt no pressure to negotiate the contents of the speech with the opposition parties.

The Harper Conservatives faced a political scene that gave them a period of security from a parliamentary defeat that could force an early election. The government could be defeated only with the help of the Liberals. But Paul Martin had resigned not only as prime minister, but also as leader of the Liberal Party. A convention to choose a new leader was scheduled for December. Until then, the Liberals, with Bill Graham serving as their parliamentary leader, could huff and puff about bringing the government down, but everyone knew they were bluffing. Until they had a new leader, they were not going to force an election.

Though free from the fear of imminent defeat, the Conservatives soon found that they would not have a free and easy run in this Parliament. The opposition parties could chip away at their program and push their own initiatives without fear that Harper would call an election every time he failed to get his way. Aside from the possibility that the Governor General might deny him a dissolution if he asked for one within a few months of the election,[35] he knew how unkind the electorate would be to a government that called an election so soon after the last one. To be responsible for a third election in a three-year period would be tantamount to political suicide.

So the scene was set for a period of rowdy, but nonetheless stable, minority government rule. The government could get much of its program done, but not all of it. From time to time Harper would be induced to adjust his program and accommodate ideas and interests of the opposition parties. Canadians would now experience a period of classic minority government rule, when government proposals have to be effectively defended in Parliament and policy-making must be opened up to include views different from those of the minority who voted for the government.

The Harper government's first budget, in May 2006, gave an early indication of how a Harper minority government would carry on. Compared with the Liberal budgets that preceded it, Jim Flaherty's first budget was a Conservative budget, featuring a lot of tax cuts. These included, besides the promised cut of 1% of the GST, significant corporate income tax cuts. But there were some clear "red" streaks in this "blue" budget, reflecting the fact that the majority of MPs—be they Bloc, Liberal, or NDP—are to the left of the Conservatives on the political spectrum. The Conservatives continued a mechanism devised by the Martin minority government (and damned at that time by the Conservatives) that would enable surpluses from the previous year to be spent on NDP priorities such as public transit, low-income housing, post-secondary education, and foreign aid.[36] Although this did not buy the two-year pact with the NDP that the Conservatives were looking for,[37] it made a government defeat on the budget far less likely. Similarly, while the budget included provision for Harper's promise of $1,200 to parents for each of their pre-school children, the deals that Martin's minister, Ken Dryden, had negotiated with the provinces to provide additional funding for institutional child care would continue for another year.[38]

In the end, the Liberals and NDP voted against the budget because it did not sufficiently address their priorities. They could afford to do so without risking an election because the Bloc supported the budget. The Bloc, aided and abetted by Quebec's Liberal government, had extracted from Harper a commitment to take the alleged federal fiscal imbalance seriously and, in future budgets, transfer more money to the provinces. With its political stock in Quebec at its lowest ever, the Bloc pledged its support for the budget twenty minutes after Flaherty concluded his budget speech.[39] So all parties were happy. The Conservatives delivered most of what they had promised. The Liberals and NDP had extracted some important concessions, and could still attack the budget for not going far enough in their direction. And the Bloc could boast about getting the federal government to admit, at last, that there was a federal fiscal imbalance that needed addressing.

Harper's number one legislative priority, the Accountability Act, was introduced in the House on April 11, 2006. It contained some of the measures he had promised for cleaning up the government in Ottawa—for instance, banning corporate and union donations to political parties, and limiting individual donations to $1,000. But by no means did Harper deliver on all that he had promised—notably, greater access to government information (for instance, to PMO documents). For the most part, the opposition supported the reforms and breathed a sigh of relief that the Gomery Commission's foolish proposals to insulate the public service from direction by political leaders had not been followed.[40] But in responding to parliamentary consideration of one of his accountability proposals, Harper showed how his leadership style would have difficulty adapting to the exigencies of minority government.

On May 16, the House of Commons operations and estimates committee examined the views of Gwyn Morgan, whom Prime Minister Stephen Harper had chosen to head a new appointments committee to be established under the Accountability Act. The appointment committee's job would be to monitor the quality of government appointments to boards and commissions. Opposition members, who constituted a majority on the committee, were concerned about troubling statements Mr. Morgan had made about immigrants and the fact that he was a prominent Conservative fundraiser. They voted to reject Morgan's nomination. Instead of working with the opposition to find a less partisan person for the position, Harper said he would not put forward another candidate until his party had a majority of seats in the House. The prime minister was of the view that, to clean up the appointment process, "We will obviously need a majority government."[41] This observer drew the exact opposite conclusion: a majority government would diminish the prospects of reducing partisanship in the federal appointments process. "My way or no way" is not a formula for governing in a minority government parliament.

Further evidence of Harper's desire to operate without significant engagement with Parliament was provided by his effort to control the appointment of chairs of House committees. As opposition leader during Martin's minority government, Harper had led a backbench rebellion that forced Prime Minister Martin to allow committees to choose their chairs by secret ballot. Now, as prime minister, he would pre-select a Conservative MP to chair each committee.[42] A government MP who ran against Harper's candidate would have to pay the cost of incurring the prime minister's disfavour. Controlling the selection of House committee chairs would not remove the opposition parties' majority on these committees, but it did signal how a Harper majority government might treat parliamentary committees.

One of the earliest concessions to parliamentary government that the opposition parties were able to wring out of Harper was an opportunity to have a parliamentary debate on Canada's military mission in Afghanistan. Although the prime minister acceded to demands to debate the Afghanistan war, he allowed little time for the opposition to prepare for the debate. Still, the fact that the debate took place helped to revive the vital role that Parliament ought to play in decisions that commit the men and women of our armed forces to engage in military combat.[43] Despite their reservations about the open-ended nature of the Afghanistan mission, all three opposition parties voiced strong support for the troops in Afghanistan.[44]

By the summer of 2006, six months into its mandate, it was evident that the Harper minority government was settling in and learning to live without a parliamentary majority. Clearly, this is not how Stephen Harper would *like* to govern. At the time, Harper continued to complain about being hamstrung by the lack of a majority. Yet, despite his grumpy hectoring, he was getting things done. When Parliament prorogued for the summer, he could check off three of his "big five" priorities—the Accountability Act, tax cuts, and his child-care plan—as pretty well done. On the other two—reducing hospital waiting times and toughening up on crime—his government faced some serious obstacles. On the first, Harper was finding what his health minister, Tony Clement, a former Ontario minister of health, must surely have told him: the provinces would insist that they needed more federal money if they were to make significant improvements in administering health care. As for the government's crime bills, they would have to win the support of parliamentarians who were less convinced than the Tories that increasing the likelihood and duration of prison sentences is the smartest way of dealing with crime.

After Parliament returned in the fall and Harper's government completed its first year in office, it was clear that the politicians, the pundits, and perhaps even the people were learning that minority government was a tolerable state of affairs. Indeed, if you have a taste for compromise and consensus, as this writer does, you might even get a wee bit joyful about it.

The most dramatic example of minority government's potential for consensus building came with the Liberal Party's choice, in December 2006, of Stéphane Dion as their new leader. Dion distinguished himself from his competitors by his commitment to environmental sustainability. His come-from-behind victory at the Liberal convention showed that a majority of Liberals want "green" leadership, and the general popularity of his victory showed that this kind of leadership would go down well with the country, too. And so, Prime Minister Harper—up to this point a skeptic about global warming and the urgency of reducing greenhouse gas emissions—suddenly became green, too. He replaced his environment minister, Rona Ambrose, with John Baird, a cabinet heavyweight, and gave him a very different mandate from Ambrose's. The Conservatives would now take climate change seriously and produce a policy that would enable them to compete with Stéphane Dion.

The Conservatives' main parliamentary ally in developing a new environmental policy was the NDP. NDP leader Jack Layton, using the leverage a minority government Parliament gives his party, pushed the government to include serious efforts at reducing carbon emissions in its proposed clean-air legislation. When Parliament returned from its Christmas recess at the end of January 2007, there were signs of the NDP and Conservatives working together in a special parliamentary committee on environmental legislation.[45] Under their new leader, the Liberals took to the attack and pushed for a clear government commitment to the Kyoto Protocol.

On February 14, the three opposition parties voted 161 to 113 to support Liberal MP Pablo Rodriguez's private member bill calling on the government, within 60 days, to present Parliament with a plan that would enable Canada to meet its Kyoto commitment.[46] Government members voted against the bill that, as a private member's bill, could not mandate the expenditure of money. Nonetheless, the prime minister said he would respect the bill and produce a plan for reducing carbon emissions.[47] Although the government's plan would likely be less robust than Dion and the Liberals would require, it would still move Conservative policy toward the political centre.

Climate change was not the only area in which the minority government situation was fostering a more inclusive approach to policy-making. On March 19, Jim Flaherty brought down his second budget, which was even more accommodating to opposition viewpoints than his first had been. Its emphasis was on new social expenditures to assist working families and seniors, and on increasing transfers to the provinces, with Quebec getting 40% of the new transfers in the first year. Columnist John

Ibbitson called it "a budget so Liberal, the Grits should sue."[48] Again—and not surprisingly, given how generously the budget treated Quebec—the Bloc immediately said it would support the budget, thus making it easy for the Liberals and NDP to attack the budget for not going far enough in their direction.

There remained a significant ideological gulf between Conservatives and Liberals on the government's package of Criminal Code amendments aimed at getting tougher on crime (one of its big five election priorities). Two of the government's crime bills had passed: one increasing penalties for street racing and the other a watered-down version of the promised restrictions on "house arrest."[49] However, several other measures—including one that would increase minimum prison sentences for gun- and gang-related offences, another repealing the right to early release on condition of good behaviour for prisoners who serve two-thirds of their sentence, and a "three-strikes-and-you're-in" for an indefinite prison term provision modelled on a controversial California law—were meeting with a good deal of resistance in parliamentary committees. Opposition MPs, like a lot of justice officials, were not convinced that significantly increasing the prison population was the smartest way to reduce crime. If the government was unwilling to go at least some way to accommodate these opposing views, it appeared unlikely that much of its "get tough on crime" program would be enacted.[50]

As the Harper government settled into its second year, political commentators were changing their tune about minority government. Enough consensus was emerging in Parliament to cast serious doubt on the need for an early election.[51] The quiet passage of Bill C-16, fixing election dates for every four years and supported by all parties, was the clearest evidence yet that the political leadership at the federal level was learning a new political discipline. Politicians sense that Canadians voters, like other democratic electorates, do not welcome frequent elections. Subject to one condition, the legislation sets October 19, 2009 as the date for the next general election. Subsequent elections will be held every four years thereafter on the third Monday in October. However, the legislation stipulates that it does not affect "the power of the Governor General, including the power to dissolve Parliament at the Governor General's discretion."[52] The one condition that could bring about a federal election before October 19, 2009 is the Governor General's exercise of her power to dissolve Parliament.

If the government were to be defeated on a non-confidence motion before October 2009, this would probably trigger an earlier election. Following such a defeat, the Governor General should inquire whether the Leader of the Opposition, Stéphane Dion, wishes to form a government. But the possibility of the Liberal leader taking up this option is remote. Securing the support of both the Bloc and the NDP—which is what the Liberals would need to have majority support in the House—is surely out of the question at this point. If the Governor General agrees to dissolve Parliament following a defeat of the Harper government, then the election would take place in the usual way a few weeks later. But the subsequent election would be scheduled for the third Monday in October in the fourth calendar year after the election.

What if Prime Minister Harper were to ask for a dissolution without having been defeated in the House? Such a request, in the view of Robert Nicholson, the Harper government's Minister of Democratic Reform, "would require perusal by the

Governor General."[53] And so it should. The legislation sched-uling elections for every four years is evidence of Parliament's intent to change the convention that has allowed prime ministers to call snap elections once a reasonable time (Eugene Forsey said a year) has elapsed since the previous election. But, even though the new legislation has removed the prime minister's power to call elections at his pleasure, there is still plenty of wig-gle room for a prime minister to engineer a defeat that could lead to an unscheduled election. The Martin minority government and the Harper minority government in its first year and a half were less eager than previous governments to regard any defeat in the House as amounting to a non-confidence vote. But it remains open for the prime minister to treat any one of the issues on which a majority in the House oppose his government—for instance, Kyoto or one of the crime bills—as a confidence mat-ter that could trigger a request for a dissolution.

With the passage of Bill C-16, election fever abated for a while. But that did not mean that the 39th Parliament had be-come a love-in. The opposition parties continued to attack the Harper government on several policy fronts. When Guy Lau-zon, the Conservative chair of the House committee on official languages, closed the committee down in order to avoid hear-ings on the implications of the government's cancellation of the court challenges program for minority language groups, the three opposition parties used their numbers to oust Lauzon from the chair.[54] They then formed a renegade committee to conduct hearings on the issue. Conflict continued on the Kyoto front. When Conservative senators staged a filibuster against the Rodriguez bill, Liberal senators threatened to block passage of the government's budget bill. In late June 2007, the lure of a summer break produced a compromise: the Senate Liberals passed the budget that Liberals in the House had voted against, and the Rodriguez bill requiring the Government of Canada to take steps to meet Canada's emissions-reduction targets under the Kyoto Protocol passed the Senate and became law[55]— with the prime minister signalling that he had no intention of complying with the law.[56] On June 22, Parliament broke for the summer, with heavy storm clouds on the horizon for its resumption in the fall.

By the end of the summer, the Harper minority government would surpass the average lifespan of federal minority governments. There was now talk of opening a new session of Parliament in the fall of 2007 with a Speech from the Throne setting out a program for a second period of Conservative minority government. Despite the sour and surly mood that prevailed in Parliament, a good deal had been accomplished in the Harper minority government's first eighteen months. Three of the big five items in the government's original mandate (accountability legislation, tax cuts, and a new child-care program) were pretty well done. On the other two (reducing hospital waiting times and enacting getting-tough-on-crime measures), about as much had been accomplished as was possible. In early April, the prime minister had been able to announce that a promise of $600 million in additional funding had extracted commitments from all of the provinces and territories to guarantee shorter waiting times in at least one of the critical areas.[57] A few of the crime bills had been enacted, while others were still at the committee stage in the House or the Senate. The government appeared to pull back from its promise to abolish the registry for rifles, a promise that—however appealing it might be to a part of its constituency—was most unlikely to ever win the support of Parliament.

In addition to getting much of its "big five" done, the Harper government could point to other accomplishments, including a veterans' bill of rights and ombudsman, a $1.5 billion trust fund for greenhouse gas reduction, a science and technology strategy to increase private-sector innovation, and a commitment to keep Canadian troops in Afghanistan for another two years—not to mention fixed-election-date legislation that can serve as an important stabilizer for minority governments.

Stephen Harper could hardly claim he needed a majority to accomplish the program on which he had campaigned in the election. To make a case for a majority, he would need to unveil a new program that only a Conservative majority government could accomplish. And that is exactly what he decided to do when Parliament resumed in the fall. In early September, Harper announced that he had asked the Governor General to end the current session of Parliament and begin a new one with a Speech from the Throne in which the government would unveil a new legislative agenda.[58]

It soon became apparent that in the new session Harper would play hardball. There was to be no more compromising or negotiating with opposition parties. On every issue, it would be Harper's way or no way; defeat on any issue would be treated as a non-confidence vote.[59] And the government was prepared to load its legislative guns so as to *invite* defeat. Its array of crime bills that had been amended and delayed in the previous session would now be brought together, stripped of some opposition amendments, in an omnibus bill that the opposition would be dared to vote down.[60]

The Harper government's sharp change of tone was clearly prompted by a decline in the Liberals' political fortunes and an improvement in its own. In the three Quebec by-elections held in Quebec on September 18, the Liberals lost Outremont (a seat they had held since it was created in 1935) to the NDP, and the Conservatives took a seat from the Bloc in its Lac Saint-Jean stronghold. Dion's Quebec troubles increased when members of the party's Quebec wing were outraged by the remarks of his national director, Jamie Carroll, who denied that the party needed to hire more Quebecers.[61] Meanwhile, Harper, in a clever move, lessened his vulnerability to attack on Canada's military mission in Afghanistan, which has been so unpopular in Quebec, by appointing John Manley, a Liberal elder statesman and former deputy prime minister in the Chrétien government, to chair a blue ribbon advisory group on Canada's options in Afghanistan.[62] On the eve of the new parliamentary session, polls put the Conservatives five points ahead of the Liberals.[63]

For the moment, Prime Minister Harper was in a wonderful, win-win political position. He could go ahead and govern on his own terms (and he seems to enjoy governing) or go into an election in which his main opponent was temporarily weakened and bloodied. And he would get lots of help from the other two opposition parties, the Bloc and the NDP, who were back to playing the old game of "political chicken"—now with the Liberals rather than the Conservative government as their target. Gilles Duceppe and Jack Layton were making it clear that their parties were prepared to vote non-confidence in the government on all kinds of issues. Thus, if the Liberals did not vote to bring the government down they could be blamed for keeping it in power and betraying their own principles for fear of an election. Stéphane Dion and his party were indeed between a rock and a very hard place.

As it turned out, the Harper government's throne speech was much softer and less hard-edged than many had anticipated. As the headlines proclaimed, it contained no "poison pill"—that is, no commitment that was so strongly antagonistic to Liberal positions that Dion would have no choice but to join in a non-confidence vote that would defeat the government.[64] The government's five priorities—strengthening Canada's sovereignty (which means, mainly, a greater presence in the Canadian Arctic), building a stronger federation, providing economic leadership, continuing to tackle crime, and improving the environment—were not matters that Liberals would choke on. The environmental proposals were so fuzzy that even Green Party leader Elizabeth May said they were too vague to bring down the government. The Liberals, too, were all for fighting crime, and when the omnibus crime bill was unveiled with four of the revived bills containing the compromises worked out in the previous session, they knew that it would not be grounds for defeating the government. So Dion's plight was not so excruciatingly difficult. He could—and did—criticize the government for failing to respond adequately to the urgent problems of climate change and poverty, but submitted that these deficiencies were not serious enough to plunge the country into its third federal election in three and a half years. He crafted an amendment to the throne speech which neither the Bloc nor the NDP could support, and then had his own caucus abstain from votes on the throne speech itself—thus ensuring the government's survival.[65]

The Leader of the Opposition took the same approach two weeks later, when Finance Minister Jim Flaherty presented the government's tax-cutting mini-budget in the House of Commons. Dion applauded the corporate and personal income tax cuts but attacked the GST cut and the failure to use more of the surplus to invest in the environment and social programs. But again, when it came to a vote on the mini-budget, the Liberals abstained. Dion said, "We will choose our time when we will decide to put this government down. It will not be today."[66]

As the Harper minority government completes its second year in office, it is governing *almost* like a majority government. But there are some important differences in its circumstances from those of a traditional majority government. First, thanks to the fixed-election-date legislation, the government cannot call a snap election any time it wishes. It is now up to the Leader of the Opposition to decide whether and when there will be an election before October 19, 2009. This gives Stéphane Dion the opportunity to strengthen his party and have an election when the Liberals are well prepared for it. Second, in this minority Parliament, the opposition parties have a majority on all parliamentary committees. Although Tom Flanagan, the Conservatives' chief academic adviser, regards committees as simply instruments of delay, those of us who value parliamentary democracy will appreciate their deliberations on legislative proposals and government policy.[67] Third, even though the Harper government seems determined to abandon the negotiation of compromises with other parties, it looks as if it will carry on with changes it made in its policy in the first session of this minority Parliament—namely, a full parliamentary debate on Canada's role in Afghanistan, taking climate change seriously, and accepting amendments to its crime bills. For a government that, even with everything going for it, is supported by only

34% of the electorate, these centrist policy adjustments will do them no harm. Who knows? There might even be some more of this inclusive policy-making before the current minority government is done.

Adding Up the Score

The only generalization that can safely be made about minority governments is that they have tended to be short lived. Table 3 summarizes the main facts about the dozen minority governments Canada has had. The average lifespan of the eleven minority governments that preceded Harper's was a year and eight months.

The short lifespan of minority governments has been their most serious shortcoming. Elections are the crucial moments in democratic politics when the people have a direct say in governance. But they shouldn't come too often. Elections every year or two can make an electorate cynical about politics and undermine democracy. So can constant electioneering by parliamentarians. Throughout the Martin minority government's year and a half, and during the first year and a half of the Harper minority government, parliamentary life was plagued by a constant sense of election jitters. Even in majority government situations, government and opposition parties will never lose sight of how their performances will play out in the next election. But parliamentary government surely works better when there is a period for policy-making and debate that is not permeated by the partisan hype that goes with the anticipation of an imminent election. Later in this book I will make suggestions about how we might stabilize minority governments and lengthen their lifespan.

TABLE 3   Canada's Minority Governments

PM and Party	Dates	Duration*	How It Ended
King/Liberal	1921–5	3 years, 11 months	Dissolution without defeat
King/Liberal	1925–6	8 months	Resigned
Meighen/ Conservative	1926	2.5 months	Defeated on non-confidence vote
King/Liberal	1926–30	3 years, 10 months	Dissolution without defeat
Diefenbaker/ Conservative	1957–8	10 months	Dissolution without defeat
Diefenbaker/ Conservative	1962–3	10 months	Defeated on non-confidence vote
Pearson/Liberal	1963–5	1 year, 7 months	Dissolution without defeat
Pearson/Liberal	1965–8	2 years, 8 months	Dissolution without defeat
Trudeau/Liberal	1972–4	1 year, 10 months	Defeated on budget vote
Clark/Conservative	1979–80	9 months	Defeated on budget vote
Martin/Liberal	2004–6	1 year, 7 months	Defeated on non-confidence vote
Harper/Conservative	2006–?	2 years and counting	

* "Duration" is the time between the time of the election that resulted in the minority government and the date of the next election or the government's resignation.

Reflecting on the fate of the minority governments we have had, we can clearly see that it is not always the fragility of minority governments that brings them down. Some minority governments have self-executed. These self-executions may be accidental, as was surely the case with the demise of Arthur Meighen's and Joe Clark's minority governments. But they can also be contrived, as was the defeat of the Trudeau minority government in 1972. Early elections may also, of course, be called by minority governments that simply hanker for majorities, as was the case with Diefenbaker in 1958 and with Pearson twice in the 1960s.

The fundamental reason for the short lives of minority governments is the mindset of politicians who view these governments as unfortunate interludes between the nirvanas of majority governments. If we are ever to have stability in the governments reflective of our divided electorates, this mindset will have to change. The support of all parties for legislation establishing four years as the normal length of parliaments is an encouraging sign that this change of outlook is beginning to occur.

The actual records of minority governments puts the lie to the myth that minority governments are feeble and cannot get anything done. Despite their relatively short duration, most minority governments were able to achieve a good deal. Only three were real duds: Meighen's very lame-duck government, Diefenbaker's sullen, second minority government, and Clark's fiasco. The other nine—including the one we are now watching, Stephen Harper's—all had significant achievements. Of course, what minority governments have achieved has depended on more than their leaders' agendas. They all have had to

find parliamentary allies, and to do that have had to accommodate the views of other parties. So, decisiveness often has had
to give way to building a broader consensus. But in a political
context where no political party is even close to being supported by a majority of the electorate, is that such a bad thing?

Although this book focuses on the federal level of government, I do not think that a study of minority governments at
the provincial level in Canada would show very different results. In 1964, Eugene Forsey reported that until then there had
been three minority governments at the provincial level—the
Norris government in Manitoba, from June 1920 to July 1922;
the Drew government in Ontario, from 1943 to 1945; and the
Bennett government in BC, from 1952 to 1953. Since then, we
have had a few more.[68] I am most familiar with the experience
of my own province, Ontario. Ontario has had three minority
governments in recent times, and all three, though relatively
short lived, were effective governments. The first two were Conservative minority governments led by Premier William Davis—
one from September 1975 to June 1977, and the other from
June 1977 to March 1981. A well-researched study of the two
Davis minority governments by political scientist Vaughan Lyon
concluded that "The conventional fears of minority government—that it will not get anything done, that it will avoid hard
decisions, and that its programme will be a mish-mash of values—were unsupported."[69] The most recent Ontario minority
government was the one led by Liberal Premier David Peterson
from 1985 to 1987. It was based on a formal written agreement
with NDP leader Bob Rae that set out a common legislative
program as a condition of the NDP supporting the Peterson
government for two years. At the end of two years, Peterson

called for a dissolution and won a majority in the ensuing election.

At present, Nova Scotia and Quebec have minority governments. Nova Scotia's minority government, led by Premier Rodney MacDonald, is that province's second successive Conservative minority government. I have not noticed Nova Scotia going to wrack and ruin under back-to-back minority governments. Jean Charest's Liberal minority government, formed after the March 2007 election, is the only minority government that Quebec has had since the 1870s. After just a few weeks in power, the opposition parties threatened to defeat the Charest government on its fiscal plans. But the Parti Québécois, in the throes of electing a new leader, backed away from this game of political chicken and the Liberal government survived. Quebec politicians, like Nova Scotia's, will have to learn a new political discipline if they are to live responsibly with legislatures created by an electorate very evenly divided in its support for three parties.

It is time now to take a look at the world of parliamentary democracy outside of Canada. Here, we will find that a different political culture prevails—and that minority government or coalition government is accepted as a normal state of affairs in most countries.

Notes

1. See R. MacGregor Dawson, *William Lyon Mackenzie King: A Political Biography, 1874–1923* (Toronto: University of Toronto Press, 1958), 358–68.

2. H. Blair Neatby, *William Lyon Mackenzie King, 1924–1932: The Lonely Heights* (Toronto: University of Toronto Press, 1963), 81.

3. Ibid., 136.

4. Roger Graham, *Arthur Meighen*, vol. 2 (Toronto: Clarke, Irwin, 1963). This rule was repealed in 1931. See Peter W. Hogg, *Constitutional Law of Canada* (Toronto: Carswell, 1997), 9.6(e).

5. Neatby, *William Lyon Mackenzie King*, 156.

6. Eugene Forsey, *The Royal Power of Dissolution* (Toronto: Oxford University Press, 1943), 192–93.

7. Graham, *Arthur Meighen*, 428–29. Graham writes that it "is something of a mystery" why Byng waited to ascertain the Progressives' intentions until after Meighen had agreed to form a cabinet.

8. Peter C. Newman, *Renegade in Power: The Diefenbaker Years* (Toronto: McClelland & Stewart, 1963), 95–96.

9. Denis Smith, *Rogue Tory: The Life and Legend of John G. Diefenbaker* (Toronto: Macfarlane Walter & Ross, 1995), 242.

10. Newman, *Renegade in Power*, 104.

11. Quoted in Smith, *Rogue Tory*, 273. Forsey had published a letter on the issue in the *Ottawa Journal*, but Smith tells us the *Journal* did not include the words quoted.

12. Ibid., 274.

13. Newman, *Renegade in Power*, 109.

14. Smith, *Rogue Tory*, 278.

15. Robert Bothwell, Ian Drummond, and John English, *Canada Since 1945: Power, Politics and Provincialism* (Toronto: University of Toronto Press, 1981), 233.

16. Peter C. Newman, *The Distemper of Our Times* (Toronto: McClelland & Stewart, 1978).

17. J. Murray Beck, *Pendulum of Power: Canada's Federal Elections*, (Toronto: Prentice Hall, 1968), 351.

18. John A. Munro and Alex Inglis, eds., *Mike: The Memoirs of the Right Honorable Lester B. Pearson*, vol. 3: *1957–68* (Toronto: University of Toronto Press, 1975), 97.

19. Stephen Clarkson and Christina McCall, *Trudeau and Our Times*, vol. 1: *Magnificent Obsession* (Toronto: McClelland & Stewart, 1990), 124.

20. Richard Gwyn, *The Northern Magus: Pierre Trudeau and Canadians* (Toronto: McClelland & Stewart, 1980), 149.

21. Ibid., 150.

22. Ibid., 90.

23. Frederick J. Fletcher and Donald C. Wallace, "Parliament and Politics," in R.B. Byers, ed., *Canadian Annual Review, 1979* (Toronto: University of Toronto Press, 1981), 46.

24. See Jeffrey Simpson, *The Friendly Dictatorship* (Toronto: McClelland & Stewart, 2001).

25. Paul Wells, *Right Side Up: The Fall of Paul Martin and the Rise of Stephen Harper's New Conservatism* (Toronto: McClelland & Stewart, 2006).

26. Tonda MacCharles and Bruce Camion-Smith, "Parties move to curb snap election," *Toronto Star*, October 10, 2004, A1, A6.

27. Brian Laghi and Daniel Leblanc, "Back from the brink," *Globe and Mail*, October 8, 2004, A1.

28. Daniel Leblanc, "Deal sends opposition projects for study," *Globe and Mail*, October 18, 2004, A4.

29. Brian Laghi, "Martin pleads for time," *Globe and Mail*, April 22, 2006, A1.

30. For an account and analysis, see Andrew Heard, "Just What Is a Vote of Confidence? The Curious Case of May 10, 2005," *Canadian Journal of Political Science* 40 (2007): 395–416.

31. Susan Delacourt and Sean Gordon, "Stronach shocker," *Toronto Star*, May 18, 2006, A1.

32. Jeff Sallot, Bill Curry and Daniel Leblanc, "The Liberals survive," *Globe and Mail*, May 19, 2006, A1.

33. Bill Curry and Gloria Galloway, "Four bills land in Senate's court after Commons vote," *Globe and Mail*, November 22, 2005, A6.

34. Susan Delacourt, "After the fall," *Globe and Mail*, November 29, 2005, A1.

35. In her memoir, former Governor General Adrienne Clarkson says that she would have granted a dissolution if the Martin government had lasted six months. The implication is that a request for an earlier dissolution might have been denied if the Leader of the Opposition were willing to form a government. See Adrienne Clarkson, *Heart Matters* (Toronto: Viking, 2006), 192.

36. Steven Chase and Brian Laghi, "Government to tap surplus for $3.3-billion," *Globe and Mail*, April 25, 2006, A4.

37. Bruce Campion-Smith, "PM sought 2-year NDP pact," *Toronto Star*, May 2, 2006, A1.

38. Gloria Galloway and Rheal Seguin, "Liberal critics want ceasefire in 'phony war' over child care," *Globe and Mail*, April 20, 2006, A8.

39. Chantal Hébert, "Battle over even before Bloc blinked," *Toronto Star*, May 3, 2006, A9.

40. Ruth Hubbard and Gilles Paquet, *Gomery's Blinders and Canadian Federalism* (Ottawa: University of Ottawa Press, 2007).

41. Gloria Galloway, "MPs grill, reject PM's picks for federal watchdog," *Globe and Mail*, May 17, 2006, A1.

42. Bill Curry, "Harper changes tune on appointments," *Globe and Mail*, April 18, 2006, A1.

43. David Bercuson, "The Role of Parliament in Matters of War and Peace," Annual Churchill Society Lecture, University of Toronto, November 24, 2006.

44. Bruce Compton-Smith, "Commitment is 'long term,' PM says," *Toronto Star*, April 11, 2006, A13.

45. Bill Curry, "Tories 'cut a deal' with NDP on climate legislation," *Globe and Mail*, January 30, 2007, A1.

46. Allan Woods, "Honour Kyoto, House tells PM," *Toronto Star*, February 15, 2007, A1.

47. Bill Curry, "Harper now says he will 'respect' Kyoto bill," *Globe and Mail*, February 16, 2007, A1.

48. John Ibbitson, "A budget so Liberal, the Grits should sue," *Globe and Mail*, March 20, 2007, A7.

49. Tonda MacCharles, "Jailers fear PM's justice overhaul," *Globe and Mail*, January 11, 2007, A1.

50. John Ivison, "Crime bills may rock the House," *National Post*, March 16, 2007, A1.

51. John Ibbitson, "Calling a spring election makes little sense," *Globe and Mail*, March 1, 2007, A4.

52. An Act to Amend the Federal Elections Act, Statutes of Canada, 55–56 Elizabeth II, section 1.

53. House of Commons Standing Committee on Legal and Constitutional Affairs, Wednesday, December 6, 2006.

54. Campbell Clark, "Opposition forms renegade official languages panel," *Globe and Mail*, May 17, 2007, A10.

55. Bill Curry, "Backroom deal ties Tories' hands on Kyoto," *Globe and Mail*, June 22, 2007, A4.

56. Les Whittingdon and Richard Brennan, "Harper warns Senate to face 'consequences,'" *Toronto Star*, June 23, 2007, A17.

57. Daniel Leblanc, Lisa Priest, and Gloria Galloway, "Critics blast PM's health targets as 'soft,'" *Globe and Mail*, April 5, 2007, A1.

58. Brian Laghi and Bill Curry, "PM to reboot Parliament," *Globe and Mail*, September 5, 2007, A4.

59. Brian Laghi and Bill Curry, "Harper's election ultimatum," *Globe and Mail*, October 4, 2007, A1.

60. Campbell Clarlk, "Harper reloads with crime ultimatum," *Globe and Mail*, October 18, 2007, A1.

61. Jane Taber, "Growing crisis forces Dion to cancel trip," *Globe and Mail*, October 4, 2007, A1.

62. Brian Laghi and Alan Freeman, "PM's choice of Manley catches Liberals off guard," *Globe and Mail*, October 13, 2007, A1.

63. Campbell Clark, "Tory majority seen as long shot," *Globe and Mail*, October 16, 2007, A6.

64. Brian Laghi and Bill Curry, "No 'poison pill' in Throne Speech," *Globe and Mail*, October 16, 2007, A4.

65. Richard Brennan and Bruce Campion-Smith, "Tories easily win confidence vote," *Toronto Star*, October 22, 2007, A19.

66. Bruce Campion-Smith and Susan Delacourt, "Liberals won't force election on economic plan, Dion says," *Toronto Star*, October 31, 2007, A15.

67. Tom Flanagan, "Dion: A man trapped in his own 'phony war,'" *Globe and Mail*, November 1, 2007, A23.

68. Eugene Forsey, "The Problem of 'Minority' Government in Canada," *Canadian Journal of Economics and Political Science* 30 (1964): 1–11.

69. Vaughan Lyon, "Minority Governments in Ontario, 1975–1981," *Canadian Journal of Political Science* 17 (1984): 703.

CHAPTER FOUR

Minority Governments Aplenty—Elsewhere

When it comes to thinking about their system of government, Canadians—like the citizens of most democracies—are not great comparativists. The foreign democracy they know best is the United States. In giving public lectures, most often to university-educated audiences, I find little understanding of the fact that the United States is not a parliamentary democracy or, indeed, of how the parliamentary system of democracy differs from the presidential/congressional US system. When foreign parliamentary democracies are mentioned, it is almost always Italy and Israel that are brought into the conversation as exemplars of what we in Canada will surely be in for if we can't count on majority government as our parliamentary norm.

In this chapter I will show that when you take a fuller look at the world of parliamentary democracy beyond Canada, two things stand out. The first is the global success of parliamentary democracy as compared with that of its chief rival, the presidential/congressional system. The second is that single-party majority governments—far from being the rule in the world of parliamentary democracy—are the exception; minority and coalition governments are far more common. When you examine these parliamentary democracies, particularly those where minority governments are most common, you find countries that have enjoyed many years of effective government, stable democracy, and economic prosperity.

Before turning to the details of foreign parliamentary experience, I would like to first clarify what distinguishes parliamentary democracy from other systems; readers who don't need this little exercise in Civics 101 should feel free to skip ahead. From experience, however, I know that even among those Canadians who follow politics closely, many have very little grasp of what follows.

Parliamentary Democracy Versus Presidential/Congressional Democracy

As mentioned earlier, when we the voters go to the polls in a parliamentary democracy, we elect a legislative assembly, not a government. The government will be led by the politicians elected to that assembly who have its confidence. When citizens go to the polls in a presidential/congressional system, however, they elect both a person to head the government and, in a separate ballot, the members of the legislature. That, in a nutshell, is the difference between the two systems. Let's unpack the two systems a bit.

In a parliamentary system, the licence to govern does not come directly from the people but from the ability to "command" (that is the technical word) the confidence of the legislature that the people have elected. In parliamentary systems, the head of state and the head of government are two different people. The head of state may be a monarch or a president elected by the people or, indirectly, by the parliament. But in both cases, the parliamentary head of state's powers are essentially formal and ceremonial. The main exception is when the head of state (or her representative) must play a role in determining which elected leaders have the confidence of parliament. Whether a parliamentary system is monarchical (like ours) or republican (like Ireland's and Germany's), the control and direction of government is in the hands of a prime minister (a "chancellor" in Germany) and cabinet ministers who are members of the political party (or parties) that have the confidence of the elected branch of parliament.

In parliamentary systems, the prime minister and cabinet members must normally all be members of one or the other house of parliament. In some of the European parliamentary systems, such as Sweden's, cabinet positions can be filled from outside parliament. But in countries based on the British Westminster model, cabinet members must either have a seat in one of the houses of parliament or secure one soon after their appointment. Back in 1894, Mackenzie Bowell, a senator, actually served as Canada's prime minister for a very short period. But since then Canadians have become increasingly democratic in their outlook—as Prime Minister Harper found out when he appointed Michael Fortier to the Senate so that the latter could serve in his cabinet. While it has never been constitutionally incorrect to include senators in the cabinet, today a prime minister invites a good deal of criticism if he gives a cabinet position to a senator.

Note that where there are two houses of parliament, one elected and one unelected, it is the elected house that is the confidence chamber. So at the federal level in Canada, it is the House of Commons whose confidence the prime minister and cabinet must maintain. Similarly, in the days when some of the provinces had appointed "upper" houses, it was the confidence of the "lower" elected house that the government had to maintain. In Australia, where the Senate, or "upper house," is an elected body, it is not a confidence chamber. The Senate there (as in Canada) can defeat government-sponsored legislation, but cannot defeat the government. This limit on the Senate's role is retained in proposals for converting the Canadian Senate from an appointed to an elected body, including the bills that the Harper government has introduced in Parliament.[1]

In presidential/congressional systems, government is structured very differently. An elected president is both the head of state and the head of government, and is elected separately from the legislature. The president is not a member of the legislature, nor are the individuals he appoints to his cabinet. The legislature—in the United States, the two houses of Congress—is elected separately from the president. The president's mandate to govern comes directly from the people and does not depend (as George W. Bush knows so well) on maintaining the confidence of Congress. The president, unless he is impeached, directs the government of the United States for four years, regardless of how little support there may be in Congress for his policies.

In presidential/congressional systems, like the American one, there is a separation of powers. Legislative power and responsibility are concentrated in the Congress, while the president, who is not a member of the legislature, controls the executive. But the two branches do not operate in isolation from one another. The American founders designed an intricate set of mechanisms through which the president and Congress check and balance each other. The president can veto legislation, but his veto can be overridden by a two-thirds vote of both houses of Congress. The president appoints ministers (secretaries of state), ambassadors, and judges, but only with "the Advice and Consent" of the Senate. The president is commander-in-chief of the armed forces and has the power to make treaties, but Congress has the power to declare war, to raise and support armies, and to call out the militia. Treaties require the concurrence of two-thirds of the Senate.

In sharp contrast to the presidential/congressional model, parliamentary government fuses the executive and the legislature. The prime minister and cabinet ministers who direct the executive branch are not only *in* the legislature, but their mandate to control government depends on maintaining the support of the popular branch of the legislature. Although opposition MPs (as well as backbench government MPs) and senators can initiate legislation, nearly all legislation is submitted to parliament by the government. If the legislation proposes the expenditure or raising of money, it must be submitted by a Minister of the Crown.

The fusion of executive and legislative power in the parliamentary system provides for more coherence in government than the checks and balances of the presidential/congressional system. But the virtue of efficiency may come at the cost of providing less freedom and debate. The virtues and the dangers of each system bear the marks of their origins. Many parliamentary systems, including ours, *evolved from* monarchical government, while the American system resulted from a *revolt against* monarchy. Our system of parliamentary democracy really began a century and a half ago, when the Crown, here and in Great Britain, agreed that government should be directed by ministers who have the confidence of Parliament.[2] Since that time, there has been an ever-increasing danger of the prime minister and cabinet dominating Parliament as monarchs and colonial governors once did.

The enormous expansion of government in size and scope has certainly contributed to executive domination of parliament. But even more important is the role that political parties have come to play in modern democratic politics. Political parties have become the great engines for mobilizing and maintaining political support. Elections in the age of mass electronic media and the cult of celebrity are essentially contests between party leaders. In parliament, party leaders are expected to keep their troops in line. Party discipline is strictly enforced, especially in the governing party's caucus. Power is concentrated increasingly not in the cabinet but in the office of the prime minister.[3] While this increase in executive domination and prime-ministerial power has been experienced throughout the parliamentary world, nowhere is it more marked than in Canada. A recent comparative study of prime-ministerial power in 27 parliamentary democracies places Canada at the very top of the table.[4]

It is when one party has a majority of seats in the House of Commons that our parliamentary system is in danger of becoming a system of prime-ministerial government. We have seen majority government prime ministers stifle parliamentary debate, stack committees, and generally shut down Parliament between elections. A prime minister's power in these situations exceeds that of a president in presidential/congressional democracies; in effect, it amounts to ruling like a president without the check and balance of Congress.

To those who believe in parliamentary democracy, prime-ministerial government is dangerous enough even on those rare occasions when the prime minister's party wins a majority of the popular vote. The next chapter will look more closely at the drift from parliamentary to prime-ministerial government. Here, I want to underscore how much worse this tendency becomes, from a democratic perspective, when the prime minister heads what I call a "false majority" government. In these situations, parliament is dominated by a government that a majority of the electorate has rejected. Indeed, as we saw in Chapter 2, nowadays these false majority governments are likely to have won around 40% of the popular vote. Prime-ministerial government in these circumstances means that, in its policy-making, the government of Canada excludes viewpoints and ideas supported by 60% of the electorate.

Elsewhere in the parliamentary world, false majority governments are much less likely to occur. The main reason for this is that electoral systems in most parliamentary democracies produce parliaments that reflect the preferences of the electorate much more accurately than our first-past-the-post system. This is not, as I have said, a book about electoral reform. However, since so much of the case against changing our electoral system is based on allegations about the dreadful things that are bound to happen when minority or coalition governments become the norm, it is important to take a closer look at these other parliamentary democracies and the kinds of government they provide.

The Prevalence of Parliamentary Democracy and Minority Government

Over the last two decades, the world has witnessed a remarkable growth in the number of countries that have come to enjoy democratic government. For political scientists, a democratic regime is one "in which governmental offices are filled as a consequence of contested elections." Using this definition of democracy, José Antonio Cheibub reports in a recently published study that 114 of the world's nation-states qualify as democracies.[5] He further reports that 45% of these democracies have parliamentary systems of government, 33% have presidential systems (that is, presidential/congressional), and the remaining 22% are hybrid systems that combine elements of parliamentary and presidential systems.

Parliamentary democracy has clearly been the most emulated and successful form of democracy. Winston Churchill once remarked that "The Mother of Parliaments combines the fecundity of the rabbit with the digestion of the ostrich."[6] Indeed, half of the 50 parliamentary democracies operating in the world today are members of the Commonwealth or are former British colonies; all were seeded by the Westminster model. Nearly all of the others are European countries whose parliamentary democracies evolved out of monarchical or ex-Communist states that, in making the transition to democracy, chose the parliamentary model.

The presidential/congressional democracies are found mostly in Latin America, with a few in Asia and Africa. Many of them have been established after periods of military dictatorship. Indeed, Cheibub argues that the greater fragility of presidential democracies stems essentially from this fact. Certainly, compared with parliamentary democracies, presidential democracies are more prone to breakdown. Cheibub's data show that for the period from 1946 to 2002, the expected lifespan of a presidential democracy was less than half that of parliamentary democracies.[7]

Presidential/congressional systems present the challenge of operating a system of government in which power is delicately balanced between two centres of power, both of which have a popular mandate. Thus far in human history, the United States is the only country that has successfully dealt with that challenge over a sustained period of time spanning many generations. It is not easy for a people new to democracy and lacking a tradition of liberty as deep as the Americans' to support a governmental system that will serve their needs through such an intricate system of checks and balances.

The parliamentary approach to democracy that puts the direction of government and the legislature in the hands of one group of elected leaders appears to be a much less challenging system to operate. And, when one party has a majority in the legislature, the parliamentary system really is a much easier one to manage. Indeed, the danger is that it may be all too easy for a parliamentary government with a majority to so control parliament that between elections it can operate virtually as a dictatorship. This danger is significantly reduced in the world of parliamentary democracy by people choosing to support a multitude of political parties and enjoying electoral systems that honour their choices. This means that most parliamentary democracies are governed not by one like-minded group of politicians who lead the largest political minority, but by coalitions of leaders of different parties or by party leaders whose government survives by securing the support of other parties in parliament.

Political scientist Kaare Strom, who has carried out the most extensive study of minority governments, shows that only 13% of the governments produced by western European and Commonwealth parliamentary democracies between 1945 and 1987 were single-party majority governments; a full 87% were either coalition majority governments or minority governments.[8] Although minority governments in Canada have always been single-party governments, this is not always the case in the parliamentary world. Some minority governments are coalitions in which a relatively large party—usually, the party with the largest number of seats in the legislature—gives cabinet positions to members of one or more small parties but the resulting coalition still finds itself in a minority position in the legislature. Just over a third of the 125 minority governments in Strom's study were coalitions. In New Zealand, since the 1991 electoral reform referendum, all of New Zealand's governments have been coalitions and most of these coalitions were minority governments.[9]

While Canada is well above average in the frequency of its minority governments, it is exceptional in having had only one coalition government at the federal level.[10] Among European parliamentary democracies, coalition governments have been the most common form of government. What accounts for this difference? It may have to do with the greater number of smaller parties in European democracies that focus on a single set of issues or interests and do not see themselves becoming governing parties. Such parties may be willing to join in coalition governments in order to have some immediate influence on public policy, even if doing so runs the long-term risk of losing identity and following. In Canada, our so-called "third parties"—like Social Credit, the CCF, and now the NDP—have usually aspired to becoming governing parties in their own right and would rather try to influence policy by using their leverage in parliamentary negotiations than by becoming a junior partner in a majority coalition government. The Progressives, as we have seen, might have formed a coalition with Mackenzie King's Liberals in 1921, but King would only let them into his government if they shed their Progressive label and became Liberals. One can imagine the Green Party joining a coalition government if it thought it could thereby help shape environmental policy. If Joe Clark's Conservatives had been smarter about saving their government's life, they might have offered a place in their government to Créditiste leader Fabien Roy. The Bloc Québécois, on the other hand, whose overriding aim is to break up the federation, is an impossible coalition partner in any Canadian government.

Majority coalition governments are generally not as friendly to parliamentary government as minority governments. The negotiations over policy and cabinet positions that establish the terms on which smaller parties agree to enter into a coalition normally take place in the days immediately following the election. Once the coalition-making deal is struck and a coalition government has a parliamentary majority, it will be in a position to dominate parliament much as a single-party majority government does. That, indeed, is one of the complaints made by critics of coalition governments in the Republic of Ireland.[11] When a government does *not* have a parliamentary majority, there is likely to be more open and ongoing parliamentary debate about policy. Minority governments foster the deliberative virtues of parliamentary democracy much more than majority coalitions.

The Performance of Minority Governments

The very large number of minority governments that have existed in the world of parliamentary democracy makes it difficult to generalize about their performance. As we saw with Canada's twelve minority governments, they were all over the place in terms of being left or right, effective or ineffective in getting things done, with or without the support of a steady legislative ally, and so on. The diversity of performance is even greater when you look at the experience of other parliamentary countries. The 125 minority governments that Kaare Strom covers in his study operated in seven northern European countries (Belgium, Denmark, Finland, Iceland, Netherlands, Norway, and Sweden), three countries with parliamentary systems based on the Westminster model (the United Kingdom, Ireland, and Canada), three southern European countries (Italy, Portugal, and Spain), and Israel.[12] Those countries cover an enormous spectrum of politics and government. Clearly, how minority governments operate in these countries will be shaped by political culture, tradition, institutional arrangements, and political contexts.

The sheer diversity of minority governments should stand as a caution against taking Italy and Israel as exemplars of minority government regimes. The electoral systems of Italy and Israel have had extremely low thresholds for party representation in parliament. This multiplies the number of parties with seats in parliament. Political leaders have responded by forming coalition governments rather than single-party minority governments. Much of their instability stems from the shakiness of these coalitions and from the crisis-laden political context in which they function. Much more relevant as examples for Canadians are the northern European countries, where minority governments are more common than coalitions, and Commonwealth countries that share with us the Westminster model of parliamentary government.

In terms of the overall stability of the political system, there is no relationship between the frequency of minority governments and political crises or instability. The countries that have most frequently experienced minority government are among the most stable democracies in the world. But stability in a narrower sense—the lifespan of governments and the frequency of elections—is another story. Here, what we have seen in the Canadian case holds true elsewhere: minority governments generally have a shorter lifespan than majority governments. Strom's comparative data on the duration of governments for the four postwar decades indicates a mean lifespan of fourteen months for minority governments. But his data are based on a definition of a change in government that includes any change in prime minister or any by-election changing a government's parliamentary status. Moreover, most of the countries he studied have constitutions requiring elections every three or four years rather than the five-year maximum lifespan that our constitution sets for the House of Commons. The mean average lifespan of single-party *majority* governments in the fifteen countries Strom studied is only two and a half years.

A better and more relevant measure of the duration and stability of minority governments is the amount of time between elections. My survey of Canadian minority governments shows that, except for Mackenzie King's resignation in 1925, all of Canada's minority governments have ended with elections. It is the *frequency* of elections that is the most troublesome feature of our experience with minority government. On this point, the record of European parliamentary democracies looks much better. The parliamentary regimes that most frequently have minority governments—namely, Denmark, Spain, Norway, and Sweden—have elections in regular three- or four-year cycles. This regularity is reinforced by laws setting fixed dates for elections. Spain, Norway, and Sweden all have fixed election dates. But it is interesting that Denmark, which leads the parliamentary league in the frequency of minority governments, does not have fixed election dates and yet has a very regular election pattern. Since 1990, Danes have gone to the polls five times, with three and a half to four years between each election.[13]

The Danish example is instructive. It shows that what is probably more important in giving stability to minority government in Scandinavia is a political culture that accepts minority government as the norm. Politicians who lead minority governments in this milieu are not constantly in an election mode, counting the days until they can have a majority. In a recent study of Scandinavian politics, British political scientist David Arter put it this way: "All in all, it is clear that minority governments work best when they are most common and there is not a strong expectation that majority cabinets will be formed."[14]

In Canada, as we have seen, minority governments have raised the very opposite expectations. Minority governments tend to be viewed as aberrations—temporary departures from the norm of majority government. The days of minority government are full of speculation about government defeats and snap elections. Minority government prime ministers squirm uncomfortably with their lack of control over parliament and salivate for a majority. Leaders of the official opposition share the same political goal—a parliamentary majority is what they, too, must have. A party leader who cannot deliver a majority tends to be seen as a failure.

The recently enacted legislation fixing Canadian election dates for every four years, beginning on October 19, 2009, should change these expectations. The fact that this legislation was introduced by the Harper government and was supported by the opposition parties is encouraging for those of us who would like to see minority government operate in a political environment that is not continually infected with election fever. I will take a closer look at fixed elections as stabilizing devices later in this book. But now, let's turn to parliamentary countries based on the Westminster model, where—in contrast to Scandinavia—minority government is more likely to be seen as a deviation from the norm of majority government.

Minority Governments in Westminster Countries

In the 19th century, when political parties were loosely structured, single-party majority governments were infrequent and minority governments were the norm. Eugene Forsey lists thirteen minority governments at Westminster between 1834 and the end of the century.[15] Palmerston, Disraeli, and Salisbury all led minority governments; Gladstone headed two. Since the beginning of the last century, British voters have returned five hung parliaments. In all cases, party leaders responded by forming single-party minority governments rather than coalition governments.[16]

The "mother of parliament's" first minority government in the 20th century was Herbert Asquith's Liberal government, which lasted from 1910 to 1915. It was formed after two elections in 1910 in which Liberal proposals to clip the powers of the House of Lords and enact legislation giving Ireland home rule were the main issues. The first 1910 election gave the Liberals 275 seats, just three more than the Conservatives. The second gave both the Liberals and Conservatives 272 seats. The Irish Nationalists, with 82 seats in the first election and 84 in the second, held the balance of power in the 670-seat House of Commons. The deep rift over the great constitutional issues of the day ruled out a coalition between Liberals and Conservatives.[17] So Asquith carried on as prime minister, leading a minority government that lasted for five years on the basis of the support of the Irish Nationalists. With the Conservatives opposed to House of Lords reform and Irish home rule, the Liberals were the only party that the Irish Nationalists and the emergent Labour Party could support. "The lesson of the Asquith administration," David Butler comments, "is that minority government presents few problems when the minor parties have nowhere else to go and when the party in power is, in any case, minded to do what the minor parties want."[18] In May 1915, under wartime pressure, Asquith's minority government gave way to a Unionist coalition with the Conservatives.

The other four British minority governments were very short-lived Labour governments. The first came after the 1923 election that produced the most even three-way division of House of Commons seats in British history: 258 Conservative, 191 Labour, and 131 Liberal. After Baldwin's Conservative government was defeated on the King's Speech early in 1924 and the Liberals showed no inclination to join forces with the Conservatives, Ramsay MacDonald formed the first Labour government. It lasted only nine months and ended after a defeat on a non-confidence motion that could easily have been avoided.

The second Labour government, again led by MacDonald, was also a minority government. This time, following the May 1929 election, MacDonald had a plurality in the House, but depended on the support of a much-diminished Liberal Party. But just as the Labour–Liberal alliance was moving toward a quasi-coalition, MacDonald's government was defeated. The Conservatives were swept back to power in the ensuing election, winning 473 of the House of Commons' 615 seats.

British voters did not return another hung parliament until Conservative Prime Minister Edward Heath called an election early in 1974 that resulted in a Labour Party plurality of 301 seats to the Conservatives' 297 in a House of Commons that now had 635 seats. Heath tried to persuade the Liberals, who held the balance of power, to join a coalition government, but when that failed he resigned and Harold Wilson formed a minority Labour government. Wilson's minority government carried on for six months, much of which was taken up with Parliament's summer recess. In September, the Queen acceded to Wilson's request for a dissolution and an October election. She might have had cause to give Heath a chance to form a government had Heath not failed to form a coalition with the Liberals a few months earlier.

Labour came out of the October 1974 election with 319 seats, just one more than a bare majority. By 1976, by-election defeats had turned the Labour government's majority into a plurality. The Labour Party's new prime minister, James Callaghan, led Labour's fourth minority government. In March 1977, Callaghan reached an agreement with Liberal Leader David Steele "by which the Liberals promised to support Labour on key votes to the end of the session in return for a prior consultation on major policy initiatives, as well as for a promise that the government would go ahead with legislation for devolution and European elections (with free votes on proportional representation)."[19] After two years, the Liberals gave notice of ending the pact, and on March 28, 1979, combined with the Conservatives to carry a vote of confidence against the Labour government by one vote.

This brief review of the UK's experience with minority government shows how entrenched the norm of majority government has become in modern British parliamentary culture. From 1910 to 1915, Asquith governed as if he had a majority; the four Labour minority governments were short-lived interludes as the Labour Party struggled to supplant the Liberals as the left-of-centre party in a two-party system. In the first two postwar decades, the British party system came close to returning to a classic left–right, two-party system, but since the emergence of a centrist third-party alternative (the Social Democrats, the SDP–Liberal Alliance, and the Liberal Democrats), the British system has settled into a multi-party system. Britain's party system in many ways resembles Canada's, with Conservatives and

Labour being the alternative governing parties and a third party, now the Liberal Democrats (who, unlike the NDP, are in the middle as opposed to on the left), consistently winning about 20% of the popular vote. Alongside these three national parties are Irish Unionists and Scot Nationalists, who, like the Bloc Québécois, represent regional interests.

As in Canada, it is the first-past-the-post electoral system that makes majority government the norm in the UK. Margaret Thatcher and Tony Blair never won more than 43% of the popular vote. Indeed, since the 1920s, Britain has had only one government that has won a clear majority of the popular vote —Baldwin's Conservative landslide in 1931. What I call "false majority" government is the norm in Great Britain. But a deep-seated belief in the merits of majority government continues to hold sway and, as in Canada, remains the main obstacle to electoral reform.

It is no surprise to find that the parliamentary democracies based on the Westminster model that have had the most experience with minority government are Ireland and New Zealand, which do not have first-past-the-post electoral systems. Since its founding, the Republic of Ireland has used the single transferable vote (STV) to elect its members of parliament. This system is based on voting preferentially for candidates in multi-member constituencies, and is the electoral system that failed to win the approval of 60% of voters—the percentage required for it to pass—in the 2005 British Columbia referendum on electoral reform. In Ireland, STV has resulted in a steady diet of coalition and minority governments.[20] New Zealand, on the other hand, did not abandon the first-past-the-post system until a referendum in 1993 approved switching to the mixed-member proportional (MMP) system, which produces parliaments representative of the people's political preferences. It is this system that Ontario voters rejected in the referendum on electoral reform held on October 10, 2007. New Zealand has now held four elections using MMP. These elections have resulted in governments that are either majority coalitions or minority coalitions.[21]

Although the electoral systems of Ireland and New Zealand since the adoption of MMP produce parliaments in which it is rare for any party to have a majority, the governments resulting from these minority parliaments are very different in character. Irish politics has been dominated by two parties: Fianna Fáil (the party of Sinn Fein and Eamon de Valera that did not accept the Anglo–Irish Treaty) and Fine Gael (which has its roots in the pro-treaty side of Irish nationalism). Since the 1930s, Fianna Fáil has won an average of 46% of the popular vote in elections, and Fine Gael 31%. The building of coalitions and management of minority governments by either party has depended primarily on securing the support of Independent members of the Dáil (the elected house of parliament), who are frequently elected from the multi-member STV constituencies. The support of Independents is secured through personal deals, often of the pork-barrel variety, rather than through negotiations with parties over legislative policy. Even in 1981, when Fine Gael and an emerging Labour Party formed a coalition, the government's survival depended on the support of one of six Independent members. Governments, once they have their support in place, act like single-party governments dominating parliament. "The Dail," comments Des Dinan, "is little more than a glorified rubber stamp for the government's legislative programme."[22]

In New Zealand, the adoption of MMP has resulted in an increase in the number of parties that win seats. Although Labour and the National Party continue to form governments, since the introduction of MMP these are coalition governments—most often, minority coalitions. A clutch of small centrist parties plus the Green Party are able to meet the 5% threshold of popular vote required for parliamentary representation. The first post-MMP period, which lasted from 1996 to 1999, was exceptionally turbulent. During this time, National's coalition partner, the New Zealand First Party, was coming apart under its opportunist and unpredictable leader, Winston Peters; the government lost its majority; and Prime Minister Jim Bolger was forced to make way for Jenny Shipley, a new National Party leader. Since then, Helen Clark's Labour Party has formed coalition governments, first with the Alliance after the 1999 election and then with the Progressives (successors of the Alliance) after the 2002 and 2005 elections. These have all been minority coalition governments that have relied primarily on the Green Party to secure majority support in Parliament. In contrast to Ireland, coalition-building and governing without a majority in New Zealand is done not by pork-barrel deal-making but through inter-party negotiations on major policy issues.

Since the adoption of a new electoral system, parliamentary politics in New Zealand has been interesting, to say the least. But despite the turbulence and sometimes circus-like atmosphere, there has been no move to reverse the decision about MMP. Instead, the focus is on managing coalitions and minority governments in ways that provide more stability and coherence.[23] Among the innovations in parliamentary government that have been tried are an Electoral Integrity Act, which reduces the incentives for MPs to defect from the party under which they were elected, and a request by the Governor General to party leaders to make public statements about whom they would support if no party were to win a majority. In addition, there has been talk of eliminating the threat of snap elections and non-confidence votes by adopting fixed election dates, despite the fact that New Zealand under MMP has stuck pretty close to its traditional pattern of elections every three years.

The most essential techniques for governing without single-party majorities have had to do with managing coalition cabinets and securing legislative support from opposition parties in parliament.[24] Pairing cabinet ministers of one party with associate ministers of another party has been a key technique in managing coalition cabinets. Coalition partnerships and parliamentary alliances have come to be based on public agreements. For a small coalition partner like the Alliance or the Progressives, this means supporting the entire government program. But for a legislative ally like the Greens, it means working out an agreement with the government on its priority policy issues and supporting the government on confidence and budgetary matters. The new kind of parliamentary politics operating in New Zealand has been tough on the small centrist parties that tend to get swallowed by their larger coalition partner. Leaders of parties in coalition governments, precisely because of their fear of the coalition coming apart, tend to impose tight party discipline on their backbenchers. That said, however, these parliamentary conditions are conducive to a much more inclusive approach to policy-making than when a single party controls parliament.

Minority Parliamentarism

In their efforts to manage minority parliamentarism, New Zealanders have looked to the Scandinavian countries that have the best track record of basing effective government on parliaments in which single parties hardly ever garner a majority of seats. Parliamentary governments in Denmark, Norway, and Sweden are either single-party minority governments or coalitions. Often, coalition governments are in effect minority governments, needing support from outside parties to maintain a majority in parliament. Although proportional representation means that a large number of parties compete in elections, only a small number—four, five, or six—are serious contenders for parliamentary representation and participation in governance. Governments are usually based on centre–right or left–green party alliances. Following Norway's 2005 election, Social Democrats and Greens formed a red–green minority coalition government, supplanting a centre–right coalition. A year later in Sweden, the political pendulum swung the other way when an alliance of four centre–right parties formed a four-leaf-clover coalition government to supplant a Social Democratic minority government that had depended on legislative support from the Greens. In Denmark, a centre–right minority coalition, formed after the 2001 election, remained in power following the election in 2005.

In these Scandinavian countries—where, as one observer puts it, "minority governments are both routine and relatively durable"[25]—parliament plays a much more significant role in policy-making than it does in the classic Westminster model. Bargaining and negotiating among government and opposition parties is a constant feature of political life, just as it has been during the life of the Harper minority government in Canada. But the difference in Scandinavia is that parliaments and parliamentarians are acculturated to minority parliamentarism and are better equipped to participate in it. Governments do not expect to control parliamentary committees. Parliamentarians are conditioned to committees playing a constructive role in hammering out policy approaches that can win majority support in parliament. Opposition parties are better resourced than in Canada to do their own policy research, and have greater access to the government's policy research. Kaare Strom calls this kind of parliamentarism "inclusionary"—and it *is* inclusionary, in the sense that it accommodates policy perspectives beyond that of the largest parliamentary party.

Minority parliamentarism may well have economic consequences. Torsten Persson's and Guido Tabellini's study of the economic effects of constitutions[26] shows that the welfare state is smaller in what they call "majoritarian countries" than in the parliamentary countries with proportional electoral systems that produce minority or coalition governments. The welfare states of the parliamentary democracies of continental Europe, all of which practise some form of minority parliamentarism, are indeed relatively large compared with other industrialized democracies. We should not find this surprising. Minority and coalition governments are constrained in developing economic and social policy to respond to the policy preferences of parliamentarians representing a majority of the electorate—and the majority of the electorate in these countries leans to the left. This has not meant that governments in these countries have been unable to make tough decisions when faced with fiscal crises. But it does mean, as Persson's and Tabellini's data indicate, that they are more likely to respond to fiscal difficulties by raising taxes than by cutting services.[27] Minority parliamentarism is more likely to result in policy that is genuinely majoritarian than in single-party majority governments whose policies respond to only the 40% of the electorate that voted for them.

The contrast between the consensual Scandinavian parliamentary model and the adversarial Westminster model should not be taken too far. In Scandinavia, as in the other European parliamentary democracies, party leaders are constantly looking over their shoulders to consider how their parliamentary alliances and legislative accommodations will affect their electoral prospects. Elections continue to be hotly contested and extremely adversarial. Party discipline within parliamentary parties that are coalition partners is apt to be tight, as caucus members are bound to observe agreements their leaders have made. The contemporary cult of celebrity and the globalization of politics that puts prime ministers on the world stage alongside presidents as national CEOs have contributed to some centralization of power in the prime-ministerial offices of Scandinavia. Still, it is interesting to note that the experts' survey puts the power of prime ministers in Denmark, Norway, and Sweden well below that of their counterparts in Canada and the UK.[28] It should also be noted that there have been efforts in recent years to revivify the parliamentary life of countries based on the Westminster model—in particular, by strengthening the role of parliamentary committees—in the hope of making parliament more than simply an arena of partisan combat in which the government and opposition contest their fitness to govern.

Adding Up the Score

Minority parliamentarism certainly has its down side; remember, I say give it two cheers, not three. It is more difficult for voters to hold governments accountable for policies that are the result of accommodating other parties' points of view. The citizens' sense that the decision of determining who will govern is their own is also lessened when the question of who will form the next government is not settled on election night but depends on protracted negotiations among party leaders. Compromise, bargaining, negotiation, and accommodating differences—the daily fare of minority government parliaments—puts a lot of people off. The media often have a way of characterizing this kind of political behaviour as showing a lack of backbone and principle. Even among Canadians, a people who are noted for their capacity for compromise, there is much admiration for firmness, strength, and decisiveness in governance.

These concerns about minority governments are voiced in the Scandinavian countries and in New Zealand, and have much to do with Canadians' uneasiness about adopting electoral systems that virtually guarantee minority government. I will have more to say about these concerns later on. But here, I would like to underscore the democratic concern we should all have about a firmer, more decisive, winner-take-all kind of parliamentary politics in countries where there are no true majority parties. When the election winner is supported by 40% or less of the people, is it right for the winner to "take all"? Surely, democracy has something to do with the will of the people. A single-party government that manages to win a majority of House of Commons seats when only 40% of the electorate voted for it can stay focused on its own agenda. For sure, such a government will be able to have its way with Parliament—no need for it to wheel and deal or make any effort to accommodate points of view supported by the 60% of the electorate that voted for other parties. But shouldn't we be concerned about how democratic such a government will be? Is being decisive and unyielding in getting its way what we want from a government that a majority of the people have not voted for? As we have seen, in Canada today, that is precisely the most likely alternative to minority government.

Though parliamentary negotiation and compromise are essential features of governing without a majority, minority governments do govern. The track record of governments in Denmark, Norway, and Sweden—the veterans of minority government—put the lie to the myth that minority governments cannot make tough decisions. They have made tough, contentious, difficult decisions on such issues as nuclear energy, opening their countries to multicultural immigration, joining the European Union, and yes, trimming the welfare state during economic downturns. These countries and others—such as contemporary New Zealand—that are frequently led by minority governments are not basket cases, crippled in their domestic policies or unsteady in their foreign policies. Nor was Britain during *its* longest experience with minority government. Indeed, Britain under a minority government was far better prepared for the First World War than it was for the Second World War under an oversized majority government. In the late 1930s, Baldwin's Conservative-dominated National Government, with a huge majority in the House of Commons, did everything it could to stifle dissent within its own ranks and in Parliament.[29] Let us not forget that majority governments can be decisive and strong in making bad decisions. And parliamentary governments led by parties that have swept to power with support from a majority of the electorate, as Baldwin's Conservatives did in 1935, will not govern well if they attempt to shut down parliament during the course of their mandate.

An appraisal of minority governments based on empirical study rather than ignorance and prejudice does not support the view that such governments lack governing capability or effectiveness. The main difference between majority and minority governments in the parliamentary world is in their methods of decision-making. The difference is fundamentally between a system in which the prime minister and the prime minister's closest political advisers dominate the decision-making process and a system in which policy-making is subject to the give-and-take of parliamentary debate and negotiations. It is to this difference that I will now turn.

Notes

1. These bills are discussed in the next chapter.
2. For a classic account, see R. MacGregor Dawson, *The Government of Canada*, 4th Edition (Toronto: University of Toronto Press, 1963), 17–19.
3. See Donald J. Savoie, *Governing from the Centre* (Toronto: University of Toronto Press, 1999).
4. Eoin O'Malley, "The Power of Prime Ministers: Results of an Expert Survey," *International Political Science Review* 28 (2007): 7–27.
5. José Antonio Cheibub, *Presidentialism, Parliamentarism, and Democracy* (New York: Cambridge University Press, 2007).

6. Quoted in Martin Gilbert, *The Will of the People: Winston Churchill and Parliamentary Democracy* (Toronto: Vintage Canada, 2006), 83.

7. Cheibub, *Presidentialism,* 136.

8. Kaare Strom, *Minority Government and Majority Rule* (Cambridge: Cambridge University Press, 1990), Table 3.2, 65. Note that Strom's study did not include Australia, India, or New Zealand, but did include Israel.

9. Jonathan Boston and Andrew Ladley, "Efficient Secrets: The Craft of Coalition Management," *New Zealand Journal of Public and Administrative Law* 4 (June 2006): 55–90.

10. There have been several coalition governments at the provincial level, including a recent one in Saskatchewan and earlier ones in BC, Manitoba, and Ontario.

11. Neil Collins, "Parliamentary Democracy in Ireland," *Parliamentary Affairs* 57 (2004): 601–12.

12. Strom included France in his study, but only the Fourth Republic, which gave way to the Fifth Republic in the 1960s. France's Fifth Republic is a hybrid system with a directly elected president who has significant governmental powers that are exercised independently of the French parliament.

13. Comparative data on the frequency of elections and fixed election dates is presented by Henry Milner in his booklet, *Fixing Canada's Unfixed Election Dates* (Montreal: Institute for Research on Public Policy, 2005).

14. David Arter, *Democracy in Scandinavia: Consensual, Majoritarian or Mixed?* (Manchester: Manchester University Press, 2006), 106.

15. Eugene Forsey, "The Problem of 'Minority' Government in Canada," *Canadian Journal of Economics and Political Science* 30 (1964): 1–11, at 1.

16. For an account of these governments, see David Butler, *Governing Without a Majority: Dilemmas for Hung Parliaments in Britain* (London: Collins, 1983).

17. Kenneth O. Morgan, "1902–1924," in David Butler, ed., *Coalitions in British Politics* (London: Macmlllan, 1978).

18. Butler, *Governing Without a Majority*, 40.

19. Ibid., 53.

20. Roland Sturm, "Elections and the Electoral System," in Brian Girvin and Roland Sturm, eds., *Politics and Society in Contemporary Ireland* (Aldershot: Gower, 1986), 55–70.

21. Jonathan Boston and Andrew Ladley, "Efficient Secrets: The Craft of Coalition Management," *New Zealand Journal of Public and Administrative Law* 4 (2006): 55–90.

22. Des Dinan, "Constitution and Parliament," in Girvin and Sturm, eds., 76.

23. Jonathan Boston, *Governing Under Proportional Representation: Lessons from Europe* (Wellington: Institute of Policy Studies, Victoria University, 1998).

24. See Boston and Ladley, "Efficient Secrets: The Craft of Coalition Management."

25. Arter, *Democracy in Scandinavia*, 99.

26. Torsten Persson and Guido Tabellini, *The Economic Consequences of Constitutions* (Cambridge, Mass: The MIT Press, 2005), 270.

27. Ibid., 272.

28. O'Malley, "The Power of Prime Ministers."

29. Lynne Olson, *Troublesome Young Men: The Rebels Who Brought Churchill to Power and Helped Save England* (Toronto: Random House Canada, 2006).

CHAPTER FIVE

Prime-Ministerial Versus Parliamentary Government

We come now to the heart of the matter. For several decades our system of government has been drifting toward a central- ization of power in the office of the prime minister. The prime minister remains a Member of Parliament, and his government's licence to govern continues to depend on maintaining the con- fidence of the House of Commons. But once that licence is secured—as it is when the prime minister's party has a majority in the House of Commons—the idea of Parliament as a place where policy is seriously debated becomes largely irrelevant. The role of the majority of MPs on the government side is to give their unwavering support to the prime minister, while that of opposition MPs is to howl and squawk about what a bad job the government is doing and proclaim how much better they would do if *their* party governed.

This concentration of power has always been inherent in the parliamentary system of government. The parliamentary system places the direction of the executive side of government in the hands of the same leaders who have majority support in the legislature. In the modern era, a number of factors have combined to make this fusion of powers a real and present danger to the democratic capacity of parliamentary government.

First and foremost among these is the emergence of disciplined and well-financed political parties whose leaders employ the techniques of mass advertising to win and retain power. This development is aided and abetted by techniques of public management that downplay the deliberative role of elected representatives and Parliament's role in holding government responsible for its decisions. Between elections, the citizenry participates in parliamentary democracy primarily through brief exposure to sound bites and talking heads on the electronic media. On top of all this is a cult of celebrity that focuses political interest on the accomplishments, failures, and personalities of leaders.

When the same handful of political leaders directs government and controls parliament, these trends are particularly unfriendly to the democratic capacity of parliamentary government. Even if we are in one of those rare periods in modern Canadian history when a national political party has won the support of a majority of voters, executive domination is a threat to parliamentary democracy. The threat is all the greater when the politicians who control parliament have been rejected by a majority of the electorate. Then we are indeed in danger of living under what Jeffery Simpson calls a "friendly dictatorship." Minority government is no cure-all, but it has the great merit of providing a better prospect of resisting these trends and strengthening the democratic capacity of parliamentary government. As Eugene Forsey put it, "A government without a clear majority is more likely to stop, look and listen."[1]

Prime-Ministerial Government

The prime minister has always been the single most important person in Canadian government. The same is true of premiers in provincial governments. John A. Macdonald, Wilfrid Laurier, Robert Borden, and Mackenzie King are landmark names in Canadian history books. But these prime-ministerial giants of the past shared power with their cabinet colleagues and depended on support in Parliament in ways that did not warrant calling their governments prime-ministerial. The transition to prime-ministerial government can be marked by the phrase *primus inter pares*—first among equals. In earlier times, that phrase was used to describe the position of the prime minister: he had more power than anyone else, but was not in a separate stratosphere. That, however, is no longer the case. In the poignant words of Jeffrey Simpson, today "the prime minister is the Sun King around whom all revolves and to whom all must pay homage."[2] Donald Savoie, another chronicler of the centralization of power, uses the term "imperial prime-ministership."[3] A British political scientist writes about the same development in the UK in a book entitled *The Rise of the British Presidency*.[4]

The Second World War was the turning point in the move toward concentrating power at the centre. As Savoie puts it, "The focus of activity and decision during the war had clearly shifted away from Parliament to Cabinet, and it would never shift back."[5] The key development was organizing the work of the cabinet more systematically. Effective prosecution of the war required that the cabinet have agendas, that it base its decisions on well-prepared proposals, and that it be kept informed of the follow-up to its decisions. The officer of government charged with the responsibility of bringing order and coherence to the cabinet's work bore the innocuous title "Clerk of the Privy Council" or "Secretary to the Cabinet." After the war, as Canadian governments turned to building the welfare state and managing the economy and the federation more deliberately, the Clerk of the Privy Council became the top civil servant and his office, the Privy Council Office (PCO), the hub of government. And the "clerk" reported directly to the prime minister.

Along with the PCO, the Department of Finance and the Treasury Board emerged as powerful "central agencies" coordinating the work of government departments, the one to apply a common fiscal and economic framework and the other to manage the expenditure of public funds. These central agencies reduced the autonomy of line departments and their ministers. But it is another central agency, the Prime Minister's Office (PMO), that has been crucial in shifting power within the executive from the cabinet to the prime minister. Unlike other central agencies, the PMO is entirely a political office. It is staffed not by career civil servants but by short-term political appointees hand-picked by the prime minister. They are the prime minister's political advisers and organizers dedicated to making the prime minister's reign a political success. The head of the PMO is the prime minister's chief of staff or principal secretary. Next to the prime minister, he (so far they have all been men) is the most powerful person in Ottawa.

The emergence of the PMO as a powerful central agency can be traced back to Pierre Trudeau. The political staff of King, St. Laurent, and Diefenbaker numbered about 30; Pearson had about 40. Trudeau's political staff, by 1972, was over 90,[6] and the number has stayed around that level ever since. All of Trudeau's successors have found that they too needed a large PMO. It has long troubled me as a constitutionalist that tax-payers foot the bill for the salaries and expenses of a hundred or so people whose primary function is to serve the political interests of the prime minister and his party. Prime ministers and their political advisers will, of course, reply that what is good for the PM is good for the government and good for the country. That, indeed, is the central tenet of prime-ministerial government. But the PMO and the centralization of power in the prime minister's office are not good for cabinet or for par-liamentary government.

Cabinet government suffers when the influence of cabinet ministers is subject to direction by political staffers from the PMO. Cabinet ministers come from Parliament and make gov-ernment responsible to Parliament. Unlike political staffers in the PMO, whose only political resource is the good opinion of the prime minister, cabinet ministers have political and gov-ernmental experience, their own constituencies, and political resources that are independent of the prime minister. Parlia-mentary government suffers when legislation and policy are part of a carefully orchestrated political agenda put together in the PMO and presented by the prime minister to the country outside of Parliament.

The key reason that Trudeau and the prime ministers who followed him have had large and powerful PMOs is their desire

legislative role of the House of Commons, that potential is much less likely to be realized when the governing party has a majority in the House and its MPs control committees. Reviewing the state of parliamentary reform in 2004 (toward the end of a long period of majority government under Jean Chrétien), David Docherty and Stephen White report that "In relation to legislation, there was less constructive use of committees than many had originally envisaged."[9] Stephen Harper, as we have seen, has reversed the one concession that Members of Parliament were able to wring out of Jean Chrétien, and has done all he can as a minority government prime minister to reassert control over committee chairs. If his party were to win a majority in the House, it is difficult to see him allowing *his* MPs to make use of recent parliamentary reforms.

Being Presidential Without a Congress

Commentators on the growth of prime-ministerial power in Britain and Canada often refer to the style of government it has produced as "presidential." There is, to be sure, some validity in this analogy. Modern prime ministers have increasingly taken on the celebrity status of the American president. They cavort on the world's stage alongside presidents as the CEOs of their countries. In Canada, beginning with Diefenbaker and Trudeau, prime ministers have adopted a style of leadership that, like a president's, seeks popular approval directly from the people rather than through their representatives in Parliament. Election campaigns in Canada are increasingly treated like presidential campaigns. Many Canadian voters would not recognize my description, in the Introduction, of what they are doing when they vote in federal (or provincial) elections—they see themselves as electing a prime minister, not a Parliament.

But the presidential analogy should not be taken too far. There is a vital difference between the power of the American president and the Canadian prime minister—or, for that matter, between a president and any parliamentary prime minister. The president of the United States shares power with the Congress of the United States, a Congress on whose approval his authority does not depend but also a legislative body he cannot control. Even when, as is occasionally the case, the president's party has majorities in both houses of Congress, the president cannot dominate Congress in the way a majority government prime minister can dominate parliament. We Canadians witnessed this during George W. Bush's first term, when we watched the White House working hard to win the support of majority leaders in Congress. The reality of sharing power is all the greater when the opposition party has a majority in one or both houses of Congress.

US presidents would drool at the prospect of having the power of a single-party majority government prime minister. Canadians need to heed Denis Smith's warning, made during the Trudeau era, that "We seem to have created in Canada a presidential system without its congressional advantages."[10] The American founders, as liberals who had rebelled against monarchical rule, were more concerned with designing institutional protections against the concentration and abuse of power than with building a strong base for executive leadership. Thus, under their Constitution, the power of an elected head of the executive is checked and balanced by the power of a separately elected legislature. By way of contrast, C.E.S. Franks, in a leading study of the Parliament of Canada, observes that the parliamentary system "is not a system of checks and balances, but of fused, concentrated, centralized power."[11]

In fact, there are some checks and balances in the Canadian system of government, but, when the prime minister's party has a majority in the House of Commons, they operate entirely outside of Parliament. The strongest of these is our federal system of government. Ironically, Canadian federalism—though designed by our founders to be much more centralized than American federalism—has turned out to be the reverse. The fusion of power in parliamentary government operates at the provincial as well as at the federal level. In contrast to governors of US states, our provincial premiers (without an ounce of Arnold Schwarzenegger's charisma) are major players in Canadian politics.

As we watch Rodney MacDonald, leader of a minority Nova Scotia government, effectively challenge the Harper government's fiscal policy, it is evident that this kind of provincial power does not depend on the strength of the premier's party in the provincial legislature. On the contrary, there is no better way for a provincial premier to mobilize political support than by taking on Ottawa. The federal government's strength in standing up to provincial power depends on the prime minister's outlook and statecraft, not the size of his party's contingent in the House of Commons. Brian Mulroney, when he was leader of a true majority government, kowtowed to the premiers, whereas Pierre Trudeau, as both a minority and majority government prime minister, resisted their decentralizing demands. Provincial power is a real check—but often a divisive one—on the power of federal prime ministers. It is no substitute, however, for the generation of policies from within the federal Parliament that are inclusive and consensual.

The other major external constraint on government is the judiciary, and above all, the Supreme Court of Canada, the highest court in our land. The judiciary traditionally has had the role of applying the rule of law to the other branches of government. This constraint is most significant when the law that judges apply to executive acts or legislation is the law of the Constitution, and constitutional judicial review became more wide reaching when the rights of citizens as well the powers of government were set out in the Constitution. That said, it is still a misleading exaggeration to say that when a charter of rights was added to the constitution in 1982, Canada moved from a system of parliamentary democracy to one of constitutional democracy. Parliaments—federal and provincial—have never been sovereign in Canada. They have always been subject to important constitutional limits, some of which have been applied by the courts. The Canadian Charter of Rights and Freedoms and formal recognition of Aboriginal and treaty rights simply widened the constitutional limits on governmental power, and—in the case of Aboriginal treaty rights—made them more explicit.

Judicial constraints on government power, including the Charter, have their limitations. The Charter has an override clause, which enables the federal Parliament (and provincial legislatures) to insulate legislation from judicial review based on sections inscribing fundamental rights and freedoms. A more serious potential limitation is the prime minister's unilateral power to make appointments to the Supreme Court. Unlike an American president, who selects candidates for the US Supreme

Court but can appoint them only with the consent of the Senate, Canada's prime minister both selects and appoints. Permitting an ad hoc parliamentary committee to question the prime minister's selection, as Stephen Harper did in February 2006, is not much of a check on the prime minister's power. Indeed, if Canada were to experience another long period of single-party dominance and ideological considerations come to dominate judicial selection, the capacity of the federally appointed judiciary to operate as an independent check on the federal government might well be in jeopardy.[12] More practically, many—if not most—of the issues that are dealt with by the prime minister, cabinet, and Parliament do not become matters of constitutional litigation.

Aside from the electorate itself, there is one other extra-parliamentary institution that can call a prime minister to account. This is the prime minister's political party. But here we should note a decline in parliamentary power. In the days when party leaders were chosen by the party's parliamentary caucus, Members of Parliament had the decisive say in selecting prime ministers. But the demands of a more democratic age have persuaded all Canadian parties to involve the party membership in the election of party leaders, either in American-style conventions or by direct ballot. While this has created a more open and participatory process, it has also increased the prime minister's power and independence from Parliament. Prime ministers who do badly electorally—and not getting a majority counts as doing "badly"—may be removed by the party faithful. But so long as prime ministers deliver parliamentary majorities, they are virtually untouchable by the party or by their parliamentary colleagues.

What About the Senate?

Canada's founding fathers did not envision Parliament as an institution in which there was a total concentration in power. They were liberal conservatives whose conception of good government called for some check on the popular branch of Parliament if their liberties were to be preserved. According to the balanced ideal of British parliamentary government that was their constitutional inheritance, Parliament had three components—the House of Commons, the Senate, and the Crown. With the achievement of responsible government, the Crown's role in parliamentary government was reduced primarily to formalities. The one remaining area where the Governor General as the Crown's representative may have to act independently of the advice of the prime minister and cabinet is when it is not clear which group of elected politicians commands the confidence of the House of Commons. But the Senate, except for the introduction of money bills, was given the same legislative powers as the House of Commons.

The Senate had two broad purposes. One was to ensure a balance of regional interests in the federal Parliament by giving equal representation to what at the time of Confederation were regarded as the three sections of the new country—Ontario, Quebec, and the Maritimes. The other was the classic role of an appointed chamber in bicameral parliaments: to act as a check on the elected branch of parliament. In the Confederation debates, Sir John A. Macdonald gave a typical explanation of this purpose of the Senate:

> There would be no use of an Upper House if it did not exercise, when it thought proper, the right of opposing or amending or

postponing the legislation of the Lower House. It would be of no value whatever were it a mere chamber for registering the decrees of the Lower House. It must be an independent House having a free action of its own, for it is only valuable as being a regulating body, calmly considering the legislation initiated by the popular branch, and preventing any hasty or ill-considered legislation which may come before that body, but it will never set itself in opposition against the deliberate and understood wishes of the people.[13]

This is the essence of the Senate's role as a so-called "chamber of sober second thought."

The Senate, over its long history, has in fact frequently performed its role as a legislative chamber, carefully considering and improving legislation that originated in the House. But its legitimacy in performing this function has been thoroughly undermined by the way its members are appointed. An appointed second chamber might have a chance of acceptance in more democratic times if its members were selected clearly and consistently on the basis of merit—the special knowledge or experience they could bring to the legislative process. But prime ministers—*all* prime ministers—have been unable to resist the tug of patronage in advising the Governor General on who should be appointed to the Senate. Many talented Canadians have served in the Senate, but the most common and evident quality of appointees is the service they have rendered to the governing party. The very long periods of Liberal government in the modern period (30 of the 41 years from Pearson to Harper) have produced a Liberal majority in the Senate. If Stephen Harper is able to remain prime minister for a few more years, he might establish a Conservative majority in the Senate. But whether its majority is Liberal or Conservative, the Senate will have neither the independence Macdonald spoke of nor the respect of the Canadian people so long as political patronage figures so prominently in the selection of its members.

Senate reform has been on Canada's constitutional agenda for decades. The most recent effort was the inclusion in the 1992 Charlottetown Accord of provisions for a "triple E" Senate—an elected Senate with effective powers and an equal number of senators from each province. The debate over that proposal demonstrated how deeply divided the country was over the structure of the Senate. While equality of provincial representation is an article of political faith in western Canada, it is anathema to Quebecers who do not accept that their province is a province like the others. To resume constitutional efforts to restructure the Senate threatens to plunge the country into another divisive round of constitutional warfare.

The Harper government is trying to accomplish Senate reform in a way that will avoid constitutional turmoil. To that end, it has introduced two Senate reform bills that rely on section 44 of the constitution amending formula that allows the federal Parliament to make changes in the institutions of federal government unilaterally. One bill aims to convert the Senate, piecemeal, into an elected body.[14] This legislation would authorize Canada's chief electoral officer to conduct a "consultation" (that is, an election) of provincial voters on registered nominees (candidates) for Senate vacancies. Presumably (although the bill doesn't say so), the prime minister would advise the Governor General to fill a Senate vacancy with the winner(s) of a provincial "consultation." The second bill would limit Senate terms in the future to a maximum of eight years.[15] If these two measures were to become law, Canada would end up with a most unusual second chamber of its federal Parliament—an assembly of legislators elected in diverse ways according to provincial law, with the greatest numbers from Ontario, Quebec, and the Maritime provinces. If the second bill were enacted without the first, a prime minister who served two consecutive four-year terms would soon be in a position to appoint all the senators.

Canadians who may not think that Harper's bills are the best way to reform the Senate need not worry. A 1980 Supreme Court decision on the essential importance of provincial participation in Senate reform casts serious constitutional doubts on the Harper government's proposals.[16] When the Senate reform bills were introduced, in the spring of 2007, the Liberal majority in the Senate refused to deal with them until their constitutionality has been tested through a reference case in the Supreme Court. And as for avoiding a major constitutional tussle with the provinces, four provinces—New Brunswick, Newfoundland, Ontario, and Quebec—have already signalled their insistence that the federal government cannot revamp the Senate unilaterally.[17] In the new session of Parliament, the Harper government reintroduced its Senate reform bills in the House of Commons.[18] The debate on second reading of these bills indicates that the Liberals and the Bloc continue to oppose the bills on constitutional grounds. So it is likely that, once again, the Liberal majority in the Senate will insist that their constitutional validity be tested in the courts.

It is just as well that constitutional issues prevent an easy passage to converting the upper chamber of the Canadian Parliament into an elected body. Before that step is taken, Canadians need to think much more carefully than they have to date about the function of a second chamber in our parliamentary system.[19] In thinking about moving to an elected Senate, it is essential to consider the experience of the only parliamentary system based on the Westminster model that has two elected chambers. The Australian Senate is that much-dreamed-about model of Canadian Senate reformers, a triple-E upper house: a body of legislators, twelve from each state, that is not a confidence chamber but, except for the introduction of money bills, shares full legislative powers with the House of Representatives. The two elected chambers are based on different electoral systems—and this difference has turned out to be of crucial importance.

Since 1948, Australian Senate elections have been based on proportional representation, a state-wide STV system. Six senators, half of each state's allotment, are elected every three years, when all the members of the House of Representatives are elected.[20] To get elected, a candidate must win one-sixth of the votes in the state. Typically, while the two large parties—Labor and the Liberal–National Coalition (counterparts of the Liberals and Conservatives in Canada)—between them take all but one of the Senate positions in a state, a smaller party's candidate is able to win the one-sixth of the votes needed to get elected. This produces a Senate in which it is unusual for either of the alternative governing parties to have a majority, and in which the balance of power is held by members of small parties, such as the Australian Democrats and the Greens. Elections to the House of Representatives are based on a preferential voting system in which voters list candidates in each constituency according to their preference. While this system reflects voter choice more accurately than our simple majority first-past-the-post system, it consistently results in a House of Representatives in which either Labor or the Liberal–National Coalition has a majority and forms a government. The majority party government then faces a Senate in which it does not have a majority but which must agree to all its legislative proposals, including its budget, before they become law.

There are two lessons Canadians should take from Australia's experience with two elected houses of Parliament. The first is that the interests and programs of political parties—not state or regional interests—dominate the Senate's deliberations. State premiers are the primary representatives of state interests on the national stage. There is no reason to think that an elected Senate would be any different in Canada. Political parties, not states or provinces, run elections; the representation of provincial interests in an elected Senate is illusory. The second lesson is that an elected Senate that is not controlled by the governing party has contributed considerably to the liberal, deliberative function of second chambers. Legislative proposals and policy issues often get a more careful and inclusive, public examination in the Senate than the government party will permit in the House. The Australian Senate has contributed to that country becoming, through its parliamentary system, a more deliberative democracy.[21]

Let me apply what can be learned from the performance of the Australian Senate to the subject of this book—the case for minority government in Canada. Looking back at previous minority governments and watching the present one, we can see that the House of Commons, under minority government circumstances, can play much the same role as Australia's Senate. The government must frequently reach out to other parties to modify its policies enough to win majority support for them in the House. In doing so, a minority government in Canada—like a majority government in Australia—is required to adjust its policies to accommodate the views of a majority of recently elected legislators. Except, of course, in Australia the accommodation is made with opposition parties in the Senate.

In contrast to Australian senators, Canadian senators—because of their non-elected status and the stigma of patronage—do not have the legitimacy required to exercise their legislative powers to their full extent. Opposition senators (who for a long time have been predominantly Liberals) may block a major new government initiative until it is tested in an election (as Liberal senators did with the Mulroney government's free trade proposal), or until the constitutionality of a proposal is tested in the courts (as the opposition in the Senate is now doing with the Harper government's Senate proposals). But opposition party senators know that most of the time their contribution should be limited to modifying and improving legislation in ways that are agreeable to a majority in the House. Opposition parties in the House are not under the same inhibition. They know (as do opposition parties in the Australian Senate) that there are limits to how far they can press their own agendas. The government, even though it is a minority, must be able to govern. The legislative agenda in a minority government parliament will be shaped by the government and will reflect its priorities. But when opposition parties in the House encounter government positions that collide with fundamental positions of their own parties or that they believe are opposed by a majority in the country, they may well try to force changes on the government. It is in these circumstances that legislative proposals and government policy are subjected to extensive review and discussion. It is also in these circumstances that the House of Commons carries out the deliberative parliamentary role that the Senate plays in Australia's Parliament, and that John A. Macdonald and the fathers of Confederation assigned to the Senate in the Canadian Parliament.

Senate reform along Australian lines is most unlikely to occur in Canada. The effort to secure constitutional amendments that would give each province equal representation in a fully effective elected Senate would, as I have said, take us into another round of highly charged, all-consuming, mega-constitutional politics that might well result in the breakup of our federation. We could much improve upon the Senate we have if a prime minister were brave and principled enough to publicly commit himself to ending patronage appointments to the Senate and agree to be advised on Senate appointments by a non-partisan council of Canadians representing all fields of endeavour. Thrilled as I would be to hear a prime minister make such a commitment, I must confess that the shock might kill me. In the meantime, we must look to the House of Commons to perform the deliberative work of Parliament. We cannot expect majority government leaders out of the goodness of their hearts to significantly relax government domination of Parliament. Change is much more likely when elections result in minority government Parliaments that force prime ministers to treat Parliament with respect and take the House of Commons seriously. Under minority government conditions, the House must come to operate not exactly like, but much more like, European parliaments that are not based on the Westminster model. In a word, this means that the Canadian version of the Westminster model must evolve.

Evolving the Westminster Parliamentary Model

Parliament, Westminster-style, has undergone an extraordinary evolution. No one invented or designed it; it is a creature of historical adaptation. This simple point should never be lost sight of. Too often we hear critics of parliamentary reform saying the Westminster parliamentary model does not permit such-and-such a reform. Certainly, there are limits to how much our parliamentary system of government can change without destroying its capacity for combining efficiency and accountability. But we should never forget that the Westminster parliamentary system has been able to endure longer than any other in the democratic world *precisely because* it has been able to evolve and adapt to changing historical circumstances.

Just think of the broad changes that have occurred in the Westminster model since its birth in medieval, feudal times. The Crown, though still part of Parliament, ceased to dominate it centuries ago. Today, the monarch and her representative act on the advice of ministers who have the confidence of the elected house of Parliament. Unelected upper houses have had their powers trimmed by law (as in Britain) or rendered inoperative by sensitivity to democratic times (as in Canada). The franchise for electing members of the House of Commons has been extended from a small group of propertied notables to universal suffrage. As the people's House, the House of Commons has become the power house of the Westminster Parliament. Leaders of strictly disciplined political parties have emerged as the managers of power within the power house. The leader of the party that can command the confidence of that House is the prime minister (a relatively new office in the long history of the Westminster model), who, together with the cabinet members he appoints, directs government and dominates the activities of the House.

Now think of the circumstances that challenge our parliamentary system today. The most important development is the one set out at the beginning of this chapter—the centralization of power in the office of the prime minister and the tendency of prime ministers to act in a presidential manner without the check and balance of Congress. The second major development is the shift from a two-party system to a multi-party system. When the voters' choice was between just two parties, one was bound to be favoured by a majority so that it did not seem undemocratic if the winning party's leaders lorded it over Parliament. But when parties that win majorities in the House are rarely supported by a majority of the electorate, a serious democratic deficit results from their leader's domination of Parliament. The final circumstance is evidence of growing public disenchantment with a parliamentary system that reduces the Member of Parliament's role to supporting or opposing a prime minister and the citizen's role to voting every few years to determine who will be prime minister.

If Canada's version of the Westminster model is to serve us well, it must continue to evolve. Certainly, it must provide efficient, capable government. But it must do this in a way that meets our expectations that government be liberal and democratic as well as efficient. To do this, it must respond to the challenges outlined above. A crucial adjustment would be strengthening the capacity of the House of Commons to review and revise the government's legislative proposals and policies. The House of Commons must evolve into playing the role originally assigned to the Senate, but which the Senate—because of its democratic deficit—is not able to perform. The aim of much of the parliamentary reform undertaken in recent decades, especially the strengthening of House committees, has been to foster such an evolution. But, under conditions of majority government, these reforms have fallen far short of their potential. It is the central submission of this book that the best prospects for evolving our parliamentary system in the direction required to respond to the challenges of our time occur under conditions of minority government.

Michael Atkinson, in concluding his survey of the condition of parliamentary government, writes that to strengthen Parliament "it will also be necessary to challenge the fundamental principles of the Westminster model with a view to guiding its evolution."[22] I am not so sure we have to go as far as Atkinson suggests. Consider two of the Westminster model's core principles. One is that Parliament's legislative agenda is primarily based on government proposals introduced by ministers and incorporating the expertise of the civil service. The second is that proposals that involve the expenditure or raising of public funds must be introduced in the House and originate with the government. Both of these principles are fundamental to the distinction between our parliamentary system and the American congressional system. I do not think it is necessary or desirable to abandon either of these principles in order to strengthen Parliament. Indeed, the second of these principles is mandated by section 54 of our written Constitution.[23]

These principles of the Westminster model have not been violated by the more activist Parliaments we have had under past minority governments or by the present minority government. The Kyoto Implementation Act, the private member's bill introduced into the 39th Parliament by Liberal MP Pablo Rodriguez, is an interesting case in point.[24] It reminds us that under the Westminster model it has always been possible for MPs who are not cabinet ministers to introduce legislation. Few of the numerous private member bills that are introduced in every Parliament ever go through all the legislative steps and become law.[25] What is unusual about the Rodriguez bill is that it challenges the government's position on a major policy issue and that it passed through all the stages of the legislative process.[26] The Act requires the government, within 60 days, to produce a plan for Canada to meet its Kyoto commitments. While it does not explicitly call for the expenditure of money, it calls for the government plan to include "spending or fiscal measures or incentives."[27] The Speaker of the House of Commons has ruled that these words do not force the government to spend money, and therefore do not violate section 54 of the Constitution.[28] A legal action has been initiated in the Federal Court to require the federal government to comply with the Kyoto Implementation Act.[29]

Contrary to Tom Flanagan, who cites the Rodriguez bill as violating fundamental principles of responsible parliamentary government,[30] I suggest that it be viewed as an example of the kind of evolution our parliamentary system needs. A majority of the MPs elected to the 39th Parliament believe that Canada should strive to achieve the commitments it made when it signed the Kyoto Protocol. But the Clean Air Act that the Harper government introduced as its environmental centrepiece did not deal with climate change. The opposition parties—particularly the NDP—worked hard in committee to amend the government's legislation, but when the government made it clear that it would not commit to the Kyoto targets, negotiations broke down. Proceeding with the Rodriguez bill was the parliamentary majority's alternative to surrendering to the government on the issue. Prime Minister Harper has indicated that he has no intention of complying with the Kyoto Implementation Act. He and his environment minister have indicated that the government has its own plan for reducing greenhouse gases. That plan should be submitted to parliamentary discussion and debate. Through debate and discussion, the government's plan might be modified enough to win approval in the House. But a parliamentary vote rejecting it would constitute a vote of non-confidence and would likely result in the dissolution of Parliament. Nothing in this sequence of events amounts to a deviation from the core principles of the Westminster model.

If, on the other hand, the government refuses to comply with the Kyoto Implementation Act and refuses to submit its own plan for parliamentary review and decision, then we are faced with a situation that is gravely detrimental to parliamentary government: the government will be initiating new policy on a matter of great importance through regulations and avoiding the judgment of Parliament. What's more, it will be openly defying an Act of Parliament and acting unlawfully. The government has already come close to doing this in terminating funding of the Law Reform Commission of Canada without rescinding the legislation that establishes the Commission. By closing down the Commission in this way, a minority government escapes the judgment of Parliament in nullifying an Act of Parliament. But governing in this way surely borders on contempt for Parliament.

Changes to the Harper government's get-tough-on-crime proposals exemplify the normal activity of legislative activism in a minority government parliament. Opposition parties have been willing to support some of the proposals when they are made less extreme—for example, minimum sentences for gun offences.[31] In challenging the government's proposals and attempting to modify them, opposition parties are not only representing large sections of the electorate who are not convinced that increasing Canada's prison population is the smartest way to "fight crime," but they are also taking positions much more consistent with the views of professionals in the field of criminology and government officials who deal with corrections. This last point illustrates the value of opposition MPs' input when the government's legislative proposals are driven more by ideology and run contrary to expert advice available from the civil service.

One change in the operation of the Westminster parliamentary model that is directly related to the experience of minority governments concerns non-confidence votes. The rule that a government must either seek a dissolution or resign when it has clearly lost the confidence of the House is so crucial to parliamentary government that it is rightly referred to as a constitutional convention—that much is clear. However, what has *not* been so clear is what constitutes a clear indication of a parliamentary loss of confidence in the government. As Andrew Heard notes in a recent discussion of this issue, while there was a time when leading authorities said that *any* defeat of a government motion or bill amounted to a vote of non-confidence, "something of a sea change" in constitutional thinking occurred in the 1960s and 70s when minority governments became much more frequent.[32] The Pearson governments lost 3 votes and Trudeau's minority government 8. The Martin government lost 40 votes, including a vote on second reading of an important bill aimed at restructuring the Department of Foreign Affairs. These precedents support the late Eugene Forsey's view that one of the "fairy tales" about parliamentary government is to regard every debatable or votable matter in the House of Commons as a matter of principle and hence of confidence.[33]

Minority government in a parliamentary system would be virtually impossible if the government's life were on the line with every motion it made. The government should be allowed defeats on issues that it does not deem important enough to be treated as confidence matters. But the government does *not* have the constitutional right to escape the judgment of Parliament by refusing to respect a motion clearly intended by a majority of opposition party members to show their lack of confidence in the government. The fact that the motion that carried against the Martin government on May 10, 2005 was on a procedural matter did not render it ineligible to be a confidence matter. Heard points out that there are clear precedents for votes of non-confidence being made on procedural motions. Moreover, the wording of the motion left no doubt that, for the opposition, it *was* a confidence matter: it condemned the Martin government for corruption, as revealed by the Auditor General, and called on it to "immediately resign."[34] If the government thought its defeat on the motion was not a real test of confidence because it had been caught by surprise and some of its supporters were absent from the House, it could have arranged to have another vote taken within a day or two. But postponing a confidence vote that it would respect for nine days and using the time to entice an opposition member to cross the floor and join the government was, to say the least, a constitutionally dodgy way to proceed.

On the other hand, opposition parties—particularly the official opposition—must be prepared to live with the consequences of defeating the government on a confidence motion. If the government decides to resign rather than seek a dissolution (as King did in 1926), the Leader of the Opposition must be prepared (as Meighen was) to form a government at least until an election can take place. If the defeat comes within months of the previous election, the Leader of the Opposition must take responsibility for forcing such an early election. This responsibility is all the greater now that the Parliament of Canada has made it clear that elections should take place every four years. Similarly, if the government seeks a dissolution, before granting it the Governor General would certainly be justified in inquiring whether the Leader of the Opposition is prepared to lead a government until the next scheduled election. The evolution of our parliamentary system has created a new discipline for the leaders of our political parties.

There are other areas in which the Westminster parliamentary system has evolved in ways that do challenge some of its core principles. A key challenge is the breakdown of the practice of ministerial responsibility. Much has been written in recent years about ministers not taking responsibility in Parliament for the misdeeds of their departments.[35] There is also increasing concern about the politicization of the public service and a breaking of the bargain between a politically neutral, anonymous professional public service and responsible leadership by elected politicians. I have not focused on these issues here because I do not see minority government parliaments contributing as much to dealing with these issues as they do to the deliberative capacity of parliament. That said, however, when a majority government prime minister cannot impose his will on the House of Commons, Parliament's capacity for holding ministers to account should increase. Let me add that, in a minority government parliament—as we saw with the Harper government's Accountability Act—reforming government administration, and clarifying and strengthening lines of accountability can be the business of parliament and not simply a prime minister's program.

Our Best Bet

Minority government is not a panacea for all that ails parliamentary democracy, but—compared with majority government—it is our best bet to take advantage of Parliament's capacity to provide government that is both liberal and democratic.

The attraction of majority government is its ability to give government a clear, firm sense of direction for an extended period of time. Majority governments give decisive effect to swings of the political pendulum. Since the 1920s, majority governments in Canada have been largely artifacts of the first-past-the-post electoral system that can effect dramatic changes in government on the basis of relatively small shifts in voters' preferences. Remember 1993, when an increase in voter support for the Liberals from 32% to 41% more than *doubled* the

Liberals' parliamentary seats and gave Jean Chrétien a strong parliamentary base for a majority government. As Eddie Goldenberg explains, these kinds of results enabled Mr. Chrétien and his advisers to work out four-year Liberal government programs.[36]

But the stability and coherence of majority governments come at a very high cost for parliamentary government. Prime ministers with majorities in the House of Commons will not allow their programs to be significantly modified by Parliament. And never mind that a majority of voters did not vote for the prime minister's party. With 41% of the popular vote, Mr. Chrétien considered that he had "swept the country."[37] Policy issues are settled in the Prime Minister's Office, with the cabinet serving as a focus group. Instead of being explained and defended in Parliament, policy is sold by the prime minister at media events. When prime ministers have a majority, government is primarily prime-ministerial, not parliamentary.

Minority governments restore vitality to Parliament, and in particular to the House of Commons, the people's House. When prime ministers do not have a majority in the House, they don't disappear. We certainly see lots of Mr. Harper, as we did of Pierre Trudeau, Lester Pearson, John Diefenbaker, and Mackenzie King when *they* led minority governments. Under minority governments, policy is still shaped in the PMO, but it is not settled there. A minority government PM has to defend his government's policies in the House and be prepared to modify them in the light of parliamentary deliberation. The policies and legislation that result from this process will take longer to emerge and, though they will deviate somewhat from the governing party's electoral mandate, they will be more inclusive of opinion in the country.

Minority government is not something we can vote for. It is a possible outcome of the votes we cast for parties and candidates at election time. For Canadians who value parliamentary government, it is a desirable outcome—not something to be feared. It would be even more desirable and less feared if we could find ways of overcoming the instability that is its greatest weakness. It is to this subject that I will turn next.

Notes

1. Eugene Forsey, "The Problem of 'Minority' Government in Canada," *Canadian Journal of Economics and Political Science* 30 (1964): 1–11, at 4.

2. Jeffrey Simpson, *The Friendly Dictatorship* (Toronto: McClelland & Stewart, 2001), 4.

3. Donald Savoie, *Governing from the Centre: The Concentration of Power in Canadian Politics* (Toronto: University of Toronto Press, 1999).

4. Michael Foley, *The Rise of the British Presidency* (Manchester: Manchester University Press, 1993).

5. Savoie, *Governing from the Centre*, 30.

6. R.M. Punnett, *The Prime Minister in Canadian Government and Politics* (Toronto: Macmillan of Canada, 1977), 77.

7. Eddie Goldenberg, *The Way It Works: Inside Ottawa* (Toronto: McClelland & Stewart, 2006), 78–79.

8. David E. Smith, *The People's House of Commons: Theories of Democracy in Contention* (Toronto: University of Toronto Press, 2000), 106.

9. David C. Docherty and Stephen White, "Parliamentary Democracy in Canada," *Parliamentary Affairs* 57 (2004): 623.

10. Denis Smith, "President and Parliament: The Transformation of Parliamentary Government in Canada," in Thomas A. Hocken, ed., *Apex of Power: The Prime Minister and Political Leadership in Canada* (Toronto: Prentice Hall, 1977), 323.

11. C.E.S. Franks, *The Parliament of Canada* (Toronto: University of Toronto Press, 1987), 265.

12. On the need for checks and balances in the appointment of judges, see Kate Malleson and Peter H. Russell, *Appointing Judges in an Age of Judicial Power* (Toronto: University of Toronto Press, 2006).

13. Quoted in R. MacGregor Dawson, *The Government of Canada*, 4th Edition (Toronto: University of Toronto Press, 1963), 305.

14. Bill C-43, A Bill to Provide for Consultations with Electors on Their Preferences for Appointments to the Senate.

15. Bill S-4, An Act to Amend the Constitution Act, 1867 (Senate tenure). The bill replaces section 29 of the Constitution Acts, 1867 to 1982, with a new section that says a senator shall hold a place in the Senate "for one term of eight years," and removes the mandatory retirement age of 75 for senators appointed after the Act comes into force.

16. *Reference re Authority of Parliament in relation to the Upper House*, [1980] 1 S.C.R. 54 (*Senate Reference*). This decision was based on a provision similar to section 44 in the British North America (No. 2) Act, 1949.

17. Joan Bryden, "Harper's bill to limit Senate terms for senators sidelined," *Globe and Mail*, June 7, 2007, A10.

18. The bill changing Senate tenure is now Bill C-19, and the bill providing for consultations with electors in selecting senators is now Bill C-20.

19. For an excellent guide to this rethinking, see David E. Smith, *The Canadian Senate in Bicameral Perspective* (Toronto: University of Toronto Press, 2003).

20. There is a provision for a double dissolution to break a deadlock between the two houses, in which case the Senate is dissolved and twelve senators are elected in each state.

21. See John Uhr, *Deliberative Democracy in Australia: The Changing Place of Parliament* (Melbourne: Cambridge University Press, 1997).

22. Michael M. Atkinson, "Parliamentary Government in Canada," in Michael S. Whittington and Glen Williams, eds., *Canadian Politics in the 1990s*, 3rd Edition (Toronto: Nelson, 1990), 355.

23. Constitution Act, 1867, sections 53–54.

24. Bill C-288, An Act to Ensure Canada Meets Its Global Climate Change Obligations under the Kyoto Protocol.

25. See David C. Docherty, *Legislatures* (Vancouver: University of British Columbia Press, 2005), 110–14.

26. The Act received Royal Assent on June 22, 2007: S.C. 2007, c. 30.

27. Section 5(1)(iii).

28. Bill Curry, "Backroom deal ties Tories' hands," *Globe and Mail*, June 22, 2007, A4.

29. Kirk Makin, "Court action presses Ottawa to obey Kyoto," *Globe and Mail*, September 20, 2007, A8.

30. Tom Flanagan, "Liberal tactics amount to constitutional back-seat driving," *Globe and Mail*, February 7, 2007, A19.

31. Bill C-10 passed third reading in the House of Commons on May 29, 2007, after Parliament, at the committee report stage, accepted amendments with the support of the NDP and a number of Liberal MPs.

32. Heard, "Just What Is a Vote of Confidence? The Curious Case of May 10, 2005," *Canadian Journal of Political Science* 40 (2007): 395–416, at 396.

33. Eugene Forsey and Graham Eglington, "Twenty-Five Fairy Tales About Parliamentary Government," in Paul Fox and Graham White, eds., *Politics: Canada*, 7th Edition (Toronto: Prentice Hall, 1991), 417–22.

34. *House of Commons Debates*, May 5, 2007.

35. In particular, see Donald Savoie, *Breaking the Bargain: Public Servants, Prime Ministers and Parliament* (Toronto: University of Toronto Press, 2003) and *The Return of Court Government, the Decline of Bureaucracy and the Fall of Accountability: The UK and Canada* (Toronto: University of Toronto Press, forthcoming).

36. Goldenberg, *The Way It Works: Inside Ottawa*.

37. Ibid., 276.

CHAPTER SIX

Stabilizing Minority Government

A clear lesson from my survey of other countries' experiences with minority government is that parliamentary democracies that have a lot of minority governments tend to get better at making them work well. Practice doesn't quite make perfect, but we *can* learn from experience—including our own Canadian experience. After all, with twelve minority governments at the national level and many at the provincial level, Canada is no slouch when it comes to the frequency of minority government.

This chapter will address both the problems that we and other countries have experienced in the practice of minority government, and possible solutions to them. Decreasing the fragility of minority government parliaments and the constant election fever that infects them is the most frequently cited problem. An implication of minority government that is also often cited as an issue is the increased likelihood of the Governor General's intervening in parliamentary affairs and the uncertainty about the formation of governments. A third area of concern is the conduct of political parties under conditions of minority government and the question of whether moderating the adversarial relationship among parties that normally prevails in the Westminster parliamentary model is possible or desirable.

The chapter will conclude with a discussion of electoral systems insofar as it is important to appreciate how moving to a system of proportional representation would do much to stabilize Canadians' expectations of parliamentary government.

Fixed Election Dates

As we have seen, the most obvious disadvantage of minority governments is that they tend to be relatively short lived. This creates instability in government and a constant state of "electionitis" in parliament and in the country. Although the recently enacted legislation fixing election dates was not introduced primarily for minority government situations, it is at least a partial remedy for the instability of minority government parliaments. Legislation scheduling elections in a four-year cycle should change the expectations of politicians and the people that parliaments in which no party has a majority cannot survive for more than a year or two.

To most Canadians, the move to fixed election dates comes as a surprise. Many have a vague feeling that fixing the dates of parliamentary elections is not quite parliamentary. So it probably comes as an even greater surprise to learn, from a recent study by Henry Milner, that Canada is in the minority among "comparable democracies" in having unfixed election dates.[1] Milner's study shows that only 12 of the 40 democracies most comparable to Canada (in Europe, the major Westminster countries, and in important stable democracies elsewhere) do not have laws setting out the dates for regular elections. And while Milner's survey does not distinguish between presidential/ congressional democracies and parliamentary democracies, when this distinction is factored into his data it remains the case that a majority of democracies with parliamentary institutions have fixed election dates.

What may account for Canadians thinking that fixed election dates are somehow unparliamentary is that the three Westminster countries they know best—Australia, New Zealand, and the United Kingdom—do not have legislation fixing the normal date for elections. What these three countries *do* have is precisely what Canada has had up to now: a constitutional limit on the maximum time between elections. Our founding Constitution set a five-year maximum life for the House of Commons and a four-year maximum for the provincial legislatures. The key clause is section 50:

> Every House of Commons shall continue for Five Years from the Day of the Return of the Writs for choosing the House (subject to be sooner dissolved by the Governor General), and no longer.[2]

Section 4 of the Charter of Rights and Freedoms extends the five-year maximum to provincial and territorial legislative assemblies.[3] The five-year limit on the life of a Parliament has been our only constitutional rule governing the timing of elections. The UK has a similar five-year rule, but Australia's House of

Representatives and New Zealand's single-chamber Parliament have maximum terms of just three years. Although Australian and New Zealand prime ministers can call upon their Governors General for dissolutions and elections well before the three-year period is up, they seldom do so; elections every three years are frequent enough. Indeed, there has been interest in both countries in moving to elections every four years. In Canada and the UK, four years between parliamentary elections has been the prevailing pattern. The new Canadian legislation mandating a four-year election cycle beginning in October 2009 solidifies that norm.

Majority government prime ministers in Canada and the UK have enjoyed the opportunity of timing elections to maximize their party's electoral advantage, but they have realized that they might be punished by the electorate if they call an early election before their government has reached its fourth year. The situation changes dramatically, as we have seen, under conditions of minority government. Prime ministers without a majority in the House of Commons have regarded their situation as abnormal and an unacceptable way to govern for a full four years. Opposition leaders who think their political fortunes are on the rise are keen to bring the government down and bring on an early election. Legislation fixing election dates every four years has its greatest purchase on minority government.

It is somewhat misleading to talk about the new legislation "fixing" the date of elections. Under the new system, dates will not be absolutely fixed the way they are, for instance, in the United States. In the US, it is an absolute, inflexible rule that presidential elections take place every four years on the Tuesday after the first Monday in November and that congressional elections take place every two years in November. But in parliamentary systems—because the licence to govern comes from having the confidence of a majority in the elected house of parliament and because it may turn out that before four years are up no party leaders can secure that confidence—there must be provision for electing a new House before four years have elapsed. For this reason, nearly all parliamentary countries have safety valves in their fixed-election-date regimes. The only exception appears to be Norway.[4]

The possibility of an election occurring before the date stipulated in the new federal legislation is provided for by a clause stating that fixing the date does not affect "the powers of the Governor General, including the power to dissolve Parliament at the Governor General's discretion."[5] The British Columbia and Ontario acts fixing election dates contain a similar clause. Not many readers will readily understand the words just quoted, so let me explain.

Under our constitution it is the Governor General (and in the provinces, the Lieutenant Governor) who dissolves the House of Commons. That power is referred to in section 50 of the Constitution set out above (and in section 85 for the provincial legislatures). Section 50 does not say when it would be appropriate for the Governor General to dissolve the House of Commons before its maximum term of five years has expired. In that sense, the power is discretionary. The norms of democracy and the principles of responsible government have long required that the discretionary powers of the Crown (including the royal power of dissolution) be exercised—normally—on the advice of ministers who command the confidence of the elected House of Parliament. But circumstances may arise where, in order to safeguard parliamentary democracy, it is appropriate for the Crown or its representative (that is, the Governor General) to act independently in exercising a discretionary power. We saw an example of this in Chapter 3 when Governor General Byng refused Mackenzie King's request that he exercise his power to dissolve the House of Commons. Constitutional experts have argued ever since about whether it was right for Byng to refuse this prime-ministerial request to exercise his discretionary power of dissolution. But no one would dispute that the Governor General has a discretionary power to dissolve the House before its lawful maximum term has elapsed. The question is: how should the Governor General exercise that power once Parliament has passed legislation providing for a four-year *minimum* term?

Let us think of a possible scenario that could soon unfold. The Harper government could be defeated on a vote of confidence well before the third Monday in October 2009 (the date the new legislation sets for the next election). In this scenario, Mr. Harper might ask for a dissolution, and Governor General Jean would grant it if it were clear that Mr. Dion, the Leader of the Opposition, did not wish to form a government and try his luck with the 39th Parliament. But in the unlikely circumstance that Mr. Dion wished to form a Liberal minority government on the basis of support that he had good reason to believe would be forthcoming from the Bloc Québécois (the only party with enough seats to give a Liberal minority government a majority in the House of Commons), the Governor General would be right to refuse Mr. Harper's request for a dissolution. In this situation, Mr. Harper would resign as prime minister (as Mackenzie King did in 1925) or, if he refused to resign, would be dismissed by the Governor General, and the Governor General would call on Mr. Dion to form a government. If the Dion government were soon defeated, Madam Jean would likely conclude that the 39th Parliament was ungovernable and, assuming that Mr. Dion asked for a dissolution following his government's defeat, she would most likely grant it.

But what if Prime Minister Harper were to ask for a dissolution and a premature election *without suffering defeat* in the House, simply because the time seemed politically opportune? When the fixed-election-date legislation was discussed in the House of Commons Standing Committee on Legal and Constitutional Affairs, the Harper government's House Leader and Minister for Democratic Reform, R.D. Nicholson, said that such a request "would require perusal by the Governor General," and added that "the Canadian public would have something to say about it."[6] There is no black-letter law that now forbids a prime minister from asking for a dissolution solely to capitalize on the misfortunes of the opposition and the government's temporary advantage. We are in the realm of constitutional convention here, and conventions are ultimately enforced politically. As Mr. Nicholson's remark above suggests, a prime minister who ignores the will of Parliament and forces an unnecessary election on the people might pay dearly for it politically. In the current circumstances, as this book goes to press, Prime Minister Harper seems inclined to abide by what should now be regarded as a convention of the constitution and not request a dissolution merely for partisan political advantage.

Fixing election dates reduces prime-ministerial power. In the past, we saw Governors General accede to the requests for dissolutions from minority government prime ministers who had not suffered defeat in the House—Diefenbaker in 1958, Pearson in 1965, Trudeau in 1968—when parliaments were well short of being four years old (see Table 3 on page 62 in Chapter 3). Now that Parliament has indicated that elections should take place every four years, Governors General will not acquiesce so readily to prime ministers who seek an early election. The new legislation also puts opposition leaders under a new discipline. Bringing down a government and forcing an election may be seen by the electorate as irresponsible if the Leader of the Opposition is unwilling to form a government. Some parliamentary democracies—for example, Germany, Spain, and Sweden—permit only "constructive" non-confidence votes.[7] A constructive non-confidence vote is one that names an alternative prime minister so that, if it carries, it both defeats the incumbent government and shows who has the parliamentary support to form a government in its place. Even without such a clause in our Constitution, opposition parties that bring a minority government down and that are unwilling or unable to replace it will have to account to the electorate for their actions.

With the dates of elections fixed by legislation to take place every four years, premature elections—although possible in a parliamentary system—should not occur very often. The electorate's wrath against those responsible for causing the early election should be a strong disincentive to those who play the game of political chicken and have their bluff called. If a premature election does occur, then the base of the four-year election cycle shifts to the year in which the premature election takes place but at the time of year fixed in the legislation. For example, if one or other of the scenarios discussed above actually occurred at any time in 2008, an election would follow in the normal way after the defeat of the government, and the election following that would be fixed for the third Monday in October 2012.

A regular cycle of elections has both practical and ethical advantages for the working of our parliamentary democracy. A four-year election cycle provides a solid platform for governments—majority and minority—to do both short- and long-term planning. Fixed election dates also enable parliamentary committees to plan their work better and avoid having their legislative policy work short-circuited by surprise elections. Voters, too, will appreciate not being surprised by elections; a number of commentators think that fixed election dates will enhance voter turnout. The parliamentarians who settled on the third week in October as the time for federal elections thought that this post-Thanksgiving, late fall season was a relatively pleasant and convenient time for Canadians to go to the polls. Henry Milner points to the potential of fixed election dates for teaching civics in schools and to new Canadians.[8] When the election is known well in advance, teachers can be well prepared to use an election as a vehicle for instruction about parliamentary democracy.

Many see the greatest benefit of fixed elections in a parliamentary democracy as bringing greater fairness to the competition among political parties. The prime minister's power to call an election at a time most beneficial to his party gives the governing party an undue advantage over the opposition. Party competition should take place as much as possible on a level playing field. Decreasing the possibility of snap elections should also make both the government and the opposition more careful about the votes they treat as confidence matters. This in turn should lead to a relaxation of strict party discipline—particularly on the government side. Finally, fixing election dates for every four years is good news for the focus of this book: minority government. With four years scheduled for the life of a parliament, the government and opposition parties will be under pressure to work out legislative strategies that will enable Parliament to get some substantial work done without being constantly on the brink of dissolution.

That last point addresses the concern that fixed-date elections will result in very long election campaigns. Without fixed election dates, parties in minority government situations must be in a constant state of election readiness; in the fourth year of majority governments, parties begin to get into election mode long before the writ is dropped. Fixed election dates simply settle four years as the norm for the life of parliaments and extend that norm to minority government parliaments. Prime Minister Harper, whose government introduced the fixed-election-date legislation, should be congratulated for a reform that reduces prime-ministerial power and enhances parliamentary democracy.

The Role of the Governor General

In parliamentary democracies, the head of state may be called upon to play an important role in the formation and termination of governments. This is true in republican parliamentary systems, where the head of state is a directly or indirectly elected president, as well as in constitutional monarchies. This is so because of the basic rule of parliamentary government: the licence to govern is commanding the confidence of the elected House of Parliament. Elected parliamentarians cannot appoint themselves to government. The head of state, guided by the confidence rule, appoints the prime minister and, if necessary, can dismiss the prime minister. If an election results in one party having a majority of seats in the elected chamber, the head of state's role in appointing the prime minister is a formality—the leader of the majority party will be PM. However, if no party has a majority, the head of state will have to determine which party leader or leaders have the confidence of the elected house. Similarly, while the head of state's role in dissolving parliament is normally a formality, there can be situations, as we have seen, in which the head of state might refuse a prime minister's request for a dissolution or even dismiss a prime minister who has lost the confidence of parliament but refuses to resign or give another leader an opportunity to form a government.

The role of the monarch or her representative in appointing prime ministers in Westminster parliamentary countries has not been regulated by formal rules. It has evolved according to the "unwritten" conventions of the constitution. In pre-Confederation Canada, the key change took place with the winning of responsible government in the 1840s, when British Governors, on instructions from London, began choosing as their ministerial advisers the leaders of the parties most likely to have the confidence of elected assemblies. So long as a two-party system prevailed, one party was bound to have a majority in the elected chamber so that the choice of Governors General (and Lieutenant Governors in the provinces) as to who should be prime minister and form a government was clear. The emergence of a multi-party system muddied the waters and, at the federal level, on twelve occasions has resulted in no party having a majority in the House of Commons.

When parliaments are "hung" in this way, the well-established practice is that the Governor General waits for the incumbent prime minister to make the first decision—either to resign or to try to form a government that has the confidence of the newly elected House. If the prime minister's party has fewer seats than its main opponent, the prime minister may feel defeated and resign right away, as Paul Martin did in 2006 and Trudeau in 1979. But a prime minister in this situation might instead decide to hang on, as Mackenzie King did in 1925, form a government, and prepare a Speech from the Throne in the hope that it will be approved when the new Parliament opens. In these situations, the House of Commons determines the government's fate. But it should be noted that there is no rule about *when* the government should meet the new Parliament and have its fate decided. Recall that the Parliament elected on October 29, 1925 did not meet until January 7, 1926, and that the vote on the throne speech (which King won) did not take place until March 2. Nor is there any established rule or process concerning what the Governor General should do if the prime minister resigns after the election and it is unclear who has the best chance of forming a government that will have the confidence of Parliament.

The parliamentary democracies of continental Europe have developed more formalized procedures for forming governments and appointing prime ministers. The greater formalization results, in part, from the fact that the electoral systems of these countries have for many years been based on some system of proportional representation, producing parliaments in which it is rare for one party to have a majority. These countries are thus well prepared for forming governments based on hung parliaments.

In Denmark, when an election results in the incumbent government (which is likely to be a coalition) losing its majority in parliament, the prime minister resigns and a "Queen's Round" takes place in which the Queen meets briefly with parliamentary party leaders to get their advice on what should be done. On the basis of the advice she receives through these interviews, the Queen appoints a "Royal Investigator," who is usually a leading politician (and who might even become the next prime minister), to negotiate with party leaders and come back with advice as to whom she should appoint as prime minister.[9] After elections in Belgium and the Netherlands, the monarch commissions an *informateur* to consult party leaders and recommend a particular leader to be *formateur*, charged with the task of constructing and leading a coalition government.[10] In Norway, if the post-election situation is uncertain, the incumbent prime minister advises the King to ask the president (that is, the Speaker) of the Storting (parliament) to act as an *informateur*. Once the president has identified the party leader with the best prospects of success in forming a government, that person becomes a *formateur*. In Sweden, the responsibility for presiding over the process of identifying the party leader most likely to have majority support has been transferred to the Speaker of the Riksdag (parliament).

Besides established procedures for the post-election process of forming governments, most of the parliamentary countries mentioned above have limits on the time that can elapse before parliament is summoned to meet after an election.[11] The Danish Constitution contains the precise rule that the "Folketing shall assemble at twelve o'clock on the twelfth week-day after the day of the election."[12] In Norway, elections are on a Monday in

September and the Storting assembles on the first weekday of October. In Sweden, the Riksdag must assemble no later than the fifteenth day after election day. The constitutions of some Westminster countries stipulate when their parliaments must meet following an election: in Ireland the Dáil must meet within 30 days of polling day; a similar 30-day rule applies in Australia, while in New Zealand, the House of Representatives must meet not later than six weeks after the return of the election writs. The New Zealand provision amounts to an eight-week rule because it takes about two weeks for the election writs to be returned. Germany also has a 30-day rule. Although the actual formation of government might not take place until after these parliaments assemble, the rules requiring an early meeting of parliaments mean that an incumbent prime minister cannot delay testing whether the government has the confidence of the people's representatives for long.

After a dozen "hung parliaments"—two of them resulting from the most recent elections—it is time to give some thought to how Canada could be better prepared for these election outcomes. One overdue reform is to put some constraints on the length of time that can elapse after an election before the newly elected Parliament meets. Such a reform is warranted not just for minority government situations. Section 5 of the Charter of Rights requires that "There shall be a sitting of Parliament and of each legislature at least once every twelve months." But surely a prime minister whose party has won a majority of Commons seats should not be able to avoid facing the newly elected for up to a year. Parliamentary democracy requires the assembling of a new parliament much sooner than that. In the case of a hung parliament, there is the added need for an early test of whether a minority (or coalition) government has the confidence of the House. Months of waiting and uncertainty—recall that Joe Clark waited for nearly five months to test his government's parliamentary support—is not good for the country or the government.

At the very least, Canada should go as far as adopting the New Zealand rule and require a meeting of a newly elected House of Commons no later than six weeks after the return of the election writs. A good case can be made for an even shorter period of time. Jonathan Boston, who studied the formation of coalition and minority governments in Europe (where the time before parliaments assemble after an election is about half of what New Zealand's rule permits), recommends a 30-day rule for New Zealand.[13] On the basis of his European research, Boston makes a persuasive case that 30 days is sufficient time for the formation of a government and preparation for its confidence test in parliament. I cannot see any good reason why Canadians should be required to wait more than 30 days to find out which political leaders have the confidence of the new Parliament their votes have created. The change would be easy to make constitutionally. Section 38 of the Constitution Act reads:

> The Governor General shall from Time to Time, in the Queen's Name, by Instrument under the Great Seal of Canada, summon and call together the House of Commons.

To this should be added the rule that after a general election the Governor General shall summon the House of Commons no later than 30 days after the return of the election writs (or a slightly longer period if 30 days seems too short). This is one amendment that can be made under section 44 of the amending formula that empowers the federal Parliament, without any provincial consent, to make changes in the institutions of federal government. Let's get on with it!

Foreign experience suggests other changes that could be effected without any formal constitutional amendment. A change in political behaviour that would remove uncertainty and make it easier for the Governor General to discharge her responsibilities would be for the leaders of political parties to be less cagey about the parties they are likely to ally with if the election results in a hung parliament. In the lead-up to the first proportional representation election in New Zealand, the Governor General asked the party leaders to make clear public statements about whom they would support in the House.[14] Such a practice in Canada would assist the Governor General in determining who should be prime minister and enhance the accountability of political parties. In Canada, where there are fewer parties than in New Zealand and the two major parties tend to be less ideologically divided, it might make more sense for the leaders of smaller parties to indicate their legislative priorities and conditions for supporting any party that forms a minority government.

In Canada, the practice of not requiring a prime minister whose party has lost its majority to resign immediately after the election eases the Governor General's responsibility for government formation. This practice also means that a ministry remains in place to serve as a caretaker government in the immediate post-election period. But there are at least two situations in which the Governor General would have to become more involved in government formation. One is when a prime minister whose party has done badly in the election resigns right after the election and it is not clear which party leader has the best chance of forming a government that will have the confidence of the new House of Commons. The other is when an incumbent prime minister, following an election, forms a minority government (or coalition) and is defeated in the House well before its four-year expiry date.

In these situations, political intelligence is needed as to the politicians that have the best prospect of satisfying the confidence rule. To obtain that intelligence in a systematic and accountable way, the Governor General might consider appointing someone to perform the role that *informateurs* carry out for heads of state in European parliamentary democracies. As it is now, the Governor General has the assistance of knowledgeable staff and consults constitutional experts. While this helps with the constitutional niceties, it does not contribute much to the Governor General's knowledge of the party leaders' inclinations. Inquiries by a widely respected and knowledgeable individual might be a useful source of political intelligence for the Governor General, and would avoid her or his staff becoming involved in anything resembling political negotiations. It is important that the process the Governor General uses in these tense situations be publicly explained. The media are bound to treat the situation as a political crisis, and many of the reporters who will cover it will be clueless about the Governor General's responsibility. A firm timetable about when the prime minister will be appointed and face Parliament would also contribute further to stability.

The likelihood of minority governments suggests another change in the conventions governing our system of parliamentary government. Two Canadian political scientists, Peter Aucoin and Lori Turnbull, recommend that Canada adopt a New Zealand "protocol" that reduces the possibility of "a diet of dissolutions."[15] Under the New Zealand protocol, when the government loses the confidence of the legislature the prime minister *advises* the Governor General that the government will resign. But the Governor General does not accept the resignation until he has ascertained whether a new government can be formed that will have the confidence of the House. It is not the Governor General's job to negotiate the formation of a new government, but to ascertain "where the support of the House lies." If the Governor General concludes that a new government can be formed, the defeated government's resignation is accepted and a new prime minister and government are appointed. If, however, the Governor General comes to the opposite conclusion, then the government's resignation is accepted and an election is called.

Aucoin and Turnbull wrote before the fixed-election-date legislation was passed. With that legislation now in place, observance of the practice set out in New Zealand's protocol is appropriate in Canada. Parliaments should no longer be dissolvable on the demand of a defeated prime minister. As I have already pointed out, following the procedure set out in the New Zealand protocol would put pressure on opposition parties to be constructive in voting non-confidence in the government— that is, by indicating the new government that the House would support if the incumbent government were defeated. Again, this is an evolution of our version of the Westminster model that reduces prime-ministerial power and enhances parliamentary democracy.

It is also a development that has the potential of increasing the importance of the Governor General's role in parliamentary government. There are republicans among us who find this implication difficult to accept. For republicans, it is difficult to accept any increase in the importance of a position that is un-elected, founded on Canada's British constitutional heritage, and represents a hereditary monarch. This is not the place to debate the monarchy versus republic issue. However, let me point out to the republicans that the track record—in terms of stability, liberty, and prosperity—of the parliamentary democ-racies that have left the head of state's position in the hands of hereditary monarchs and their representatives is impressive. Electing the head of state in a parliamentary democracy—either directly by the people or indirectly by parliament—runs the risk of engaging candidates in a political process, thus reducing the likelihood that the elected president will have no partisan asso-ciations. The head of state's function in resolving the political crises that arise when it is not clear who commands parliament's confidence will be best performed by a person who is seen to be non-partisan. That is why we should question the wisdom of Canadian prime ministers who have appointed former poli-ticians to the Governor General's position. My own association with recent Governors General, who have not been former politicians, leads me to believe that Canadians have much to lose and nothing to gain as a parliamentary democracy by suc-cumbing to republican sentiment.

Agreements Between Parties

Formal written agreements between parties can certainly bring a measure of stability to a minority government parliament. Typically, these agreements amount to a smaller party agreeing to support the government on confidence votes in return for the government's legislative program satisfying some of the party's key policy priorities. The legislative alliances that result from such agreements are to be distinguished from government coalitions in which several parties form a government together and members of the different parties that make up the coalition hold cabinet positions.

Minority governments in Europe frequently have formal alliances with other parties in parliament, but a majority of the minority governments covered in Kaare Strom's study did not depend on formal legislative alliances.[16] Legislative alliances, as well as government coalitions, have become a feature of New Zealand parliamentary life under its new electoral system. As noted earlier, the Greens have made legislative agreements with minority coalition governments in New Zealand. In Canada, we have experienced only one formal legislative alliance thus far— and that was at the provincial level, in Ontario.

The Ontario election held on May 2, 1985 produced a legislative assembly in which the Conservatives—who had governed Ontario since 1943—held 52 seats, the Liberals 48, and the NDP 25. After the election, Premier Frank Miller began to put together a new government amid much speculation that it would likely be defeated by the combined forces of the Liberals and the NDP. The speculation ended on May 28, when Liberal Leader David Peterson and NDP Leader Bob Rae signed "An agreement for a reform minority parliament."[17] The agreement set out the conditions under which the NDP, for a period of two years, would agree neither to move nor vote non-confidence in a Liberal government. After a great deal of huffing and puffing about the agreement being constitutionally dubious, on June 19, Premier Miller submitted his government's resignation to Lieutenant Governor Paul Aird, who then called upon David

Peterson to form a government.[18] Premier Peterson agreed to meet the newly elected legislature on July 2—two months after the election.

The Peterson–Rae agreement was Canada's pioneer effort at using a formal legislative alliance to stabilize a minority government. It is worth examining in some detail. One point to be cleared up is that there was no constitutional problem with the agreement. The Liberal leader undertook not to request a dissolution unless his government was defeated "on a specifically-framed motion of no confidence" and the NDP leader agreed not to move or support such a non-confidence vote for two years. The two leaders further agreed that, while "individual bills, including budget bills" would not be treated as confidence matters, "the overall budgetary policy of the Government, including the votes on supply" would be. There is no constitutional bar to a prime minister announcing his intention not to seek an early election or to parliamentary leaders—including the leader of the government party—declaring in advance how they will treat non-confidence motions. One lawyer who evidently had no understanding of the political agreements and conventions that regulate parliamentary government thought that the agreement was "highly suspect" from a legal perspective.[19] But Eugene Forsey pronounced the agreement to be "impeccable"[20] and a number of other scholars in the field gave it their seal of approval.

The agreement contained proposals to strengthen, in various ways, parliamentary democracy in Ontario. These included commitments to broaden the role of House committees and public involvement in the legislative process. The package of policy reforms, all based on "common campaign proposals," was wide ranging. It included the implementation of full funding to the Catholic separate schools, legislation for equal pay for work of equal value in both the private and public sector, various environmental measures, and reform of daycare and services to the elderly. All of this was to be carried out "within a framework of fiscal responsibility." The program was highly aspirational—some of it got done, and some of it did not. But it did give Ontario two years of productive and stable minority government, and strengthened the legislative role of the legislative assembly. And it did not do much to dampen the adversarial nature of politics in the legislative assembly; the Progressive Conservatives in opposition made sure of that. The Liberals did not wait long after the agreement's two years were up to call an election. The results of the September 10, 1987 election suggest that the Liberals benefited more than the NDP from the agreement: the Liberals took 95 seats in an expanded House of 130 members (with only 47% of the popular vote), while the NDP won only 19 seats, two more than the Progressive Conservatives.

In Canada, political parties faced with the challenge of stabilizing governments responsible to parliaments in which no party has a majority are far more likely to negotiate legislative agreements than to construct coalition governments. The idea of sharing cabinet power with another party is a very uncongenial idea to Conservatives and Liberals. Smaller parties, like the NDP, harbour hopes of becoming governing parties and fear that they will lose their separate identity if they became junior partners in a coalition with a larger party. This situation might change, as it did in New Zealand, with the adoption of some form of proportional representation and the emergence of two or three new small parties whose main aim is to influence government; a centrist liberal party or a more fundamentalist conservative party might be available for coalition partnerships. Coalitions can bring as much—or more—governmental stability to "hung" parliaments than legislative alliances. But parliamentary democracy is apt to pay a high price for this kind of stability. Keeping a coalition government together requires the imposition of tight discipline on members of the governing parties. The danger of executive domination of parliament is reduced if the coalition—as has been the case in New Zealand—is in a minority position and must negotiate with other parties in parliament to obtain majority support for its policies.

At the federal level, formal legislative alliances like the Peterson–Rae agreement are most likely to be between the Liberals and NDP. Since the 1920s, the Liberals have had natural parliamentary allies to the left. King managed minority government with the help of the Progressives and some Labour members, while Pearson and Trudeau counted on the NDP to support their minority governments. The Harper Conservatives, like the Diefenbaker and Clark Progressive Conservatives, have had no obvious party to ally with in Parliament. They prefer to work on an ad hoc basis, finding the support they need on each issue from different sections of the opposition benches. On Quebec nationalism (recognizing Quebec as a nation) and devolution of power to the provinces, they can look to the Bloc. On reducing carbon emissions, they have negotiated mostly with the NDP, who may be more moderate on this issue because they must keep in mind the auto workers' concerns about job losses resulting from a full monty approach to Kyoto. On the budget and Afghanistan, it is Liberals who might support their positions. With two years of fairly productive minority government under their belt, the Conservatives have shown that they are pretty deft at this kind of parliamentary stickhandling.

Although the present Parliament is not likely to see any formal inter-party agreements, all parties should be prepared to consider them as possibilities in future Parliaments. For smaller parties, they should be seen as strategic opportunities to secure vital priorities by negotiating with a larger party that needs external support to form a government. For the Conservatives—and particularly the Liberals—legislative agreements should be seen as a good Plan B if they do not get the election results they need for their Plan A (which will always be majority government). An important lesson from the 1985 Ontario episode is: be prepared. With a Plan B in its hip pocket, it should not take two months for a potential governing party to work out a formal legislative alliance with a smaller party.

The Ultimate Stabilizer—Electoral Reform

Nothing would do more to prepare Canada's political parties for minority government than electoral reform. In Chapter 2, I explained that this is not a book about electoral reform. However, it is a book that addresses one of the principal arguments relied on by defenders of the existing first-past-the-post plurality system—namely, that an electoral system that distributes parliamentary seats to political parties roughly in proportion to the popularity of those parties with the voters would almost guarantee minority government, and minority government is a bad thing. The first part of the argument is certainly correct: international experience makes it clear that single-party majority governments are rare in the vast majority of parliamentary democracies that do not have first-past-the-post systems.[21] The results of Canadian federal elections indicate that, under an electoral system that represented parties in Parliament according to their strength in the country, Canada would have had at most three single-party majority governments since 1921.[22] It is the second part of the argument—the view that minority government is something to be avoided—that I believe is wrong and that I have tried to counter in previous chapters. Here, I wish only to underscore that one of the benefits of electoral reform is the stability it would bring to the operation of minority government.

Political leaders who compete for parliamentary seats in systems of proportional representation—including mixed-member proportional systems like Germany's and New Zealand's—know that they are very unlikely to win a majority of seats even if they run very successful election campaigns. Therefore, they are more deliberate and strategic in seeking out parties they might ally with in government. Some of these party alliances may become evident in the election campaign. Larger parties that believe they can win a plurality of seats or close to a plurality will be on the lookout for government or legislative allies. Smaller parties will also be thinking about their best strategic options in terms of allying with one of the larger parties. The structure of party competition in countries with some form of proportional representation is often between groupings of parties on the left and right. When the votes are counted, it is usually pretty clear which of the groupings has garnered the most seats and will form the parliamentary base for a coalition or minority government. Parties competing in this kind of politics are better prepared to deal with the inter-party negotiations that are required for the formation and management of minority government.

I fully realize that what I have just written will go down very badly for those who prefer majority government to minority government. While they may well be able to accept a minority government once in a while, they are apt to be repelled by the prospect of a steady diet of minority or coalition governments. The virtual certainty of that prospect under proportional representation will continue to be their main reason for sticking with our existing electoral system, the only system that can deliver frequent single-party majority governments. My appeal to those who have such a deep preference for majority government is to give parliamentary government—as opposed to prime-ministerial government—a chance, and to appreciate how minority government gives us the best opportunity to enjoy the virtues of parliamentary government. The preceding chapter was devoted to advancing that thesis. In the final chapter of this book, I want to say more about what I call the virtues of parliamentary government and how they are best sustained.

Notes

1. Henry Milner, *Fixing Canada's Unfixed Election Dates* 6, IRPP Policy Matters, Institute for Research on Public Policy, Montreal, 2005.

2. Constitution Act, 1867, section 50; section 85 sets the four-year maximum for provincial legislatures.

3. Canadian Charter of Rights and Freedoms, section 4(1). Section 4(2) of the Charter provides that "[i]n time of real or apprehended war, invasion or insurrection" Parliaments can continue beyond five years unless one third of their members oppose such an extension.

4. Milner, *Fixing Canada's Unfixed Election Dates*, 14.

5. An Act to amend the Canada Elections Act, section 1.

6. Standing Committee on Legal and Constitutional Affairs, Wednesday, December 6, 2006.

7. Jonathan Boston, *Governing Under Proportional Representation: Lessons from Europe* (Wellington, New Zealand: Institute of Policy Studies, Victoria University, 1998), 24.

8. Milner, *Fixing Canada's Unfixed Election Dates*, 24.

9. See Boston *Governing Under Proportional Representation*, 34–36.

10. See Butler, *Governing Without a Majority*, 60–61.

11. See Boston, *Governing Under Proportional Representation*, 36–39.

12. Quoted ibid., 37.

13. Ibid., 102–4.

14. Jonathan Boston and Andrew Ladley, "Efficient Secrets: The Craft of Coalition Management," *New Zealand Journal of Public and Administrative Law* 4 (June 2006): 55–90, at 59–60.

15. Peter Aucoin and Lori Turnbull, "Removing the Virtual Right of First Ministers to Demand Dissolution," *Canadian Parliamentary Review* (Summer 2004): 16–19.

16. Kaare Strom, *Minority Government and Majority Rule* (Cambridge: Cambridge University Press, 1990), 61–62.

17. John Cruikshank, "Liberals, NDP sign 2-year deal," *Globe and Mail*, May 29, 1985, A1.

18. Robert Stephens and Murray Campbell, "Aird calls on Liberals to form a government," *Globe and Mail*, June 20, 1985, A1.

19. The lawyer was Morris Manning. For his and other comments, see *Toronto Star*, June 1, 1985, B4.

20. Joe O'Donnell, "Agreement 'impeccable,' Forsey says," *Toronto Star*, May 29, 1985.

21. For an excellent account of electoral reforms and their consequences, see Dennis Pilon, *The Politics of Voting: Reforming Canada's Electoral System* (Toronto: Emond Montgomery, 2007).

22. Voters might well behave differently under a different electoral system. But the difference is likely to be a greater willingness to support smaller parties, and that change decreases the likelihood of any one party gaining 50% or more of the seats in the House.

CHAPTER SEVEN

Sustaining Parliamentary Democracy

The genius of parliamentary government is its capacity for combining efficiency and liberty. By giving the direction of the executive branch of government to the political leaders with the most support in the elected legislature, the parliamentary system provides a basis for government that is both effective and accountable to the people's representatives. Worldwide, the parliamentary system of representative democracy has outperformed its main institutional rival, the presidential/congressional system, by a wide margin.[1] The United States is the only country that has been successful over a sustained period of time in managing a system in which the executive and legislature are separate powers with their own electoral bases. Our own parliamentary system is one of the oldest in world history; for over a century and a half, it has done us well. But today it is in trouble—double trouble.

One kind of trouble has been referred to frequently in previous chapters: the danger of parliamentary government turning into prime-ministerial government. The main force behind the trend toward prime-ministerial government has been the emergence of strong, well-disciplined political parties as the instruments for winning parliamentary elections. The leader of a party that manages to win a majority of seats in a parliamentary election is inclined to virtually shut parliament down until the next election. When that happens, the efficiency aspect of the parliamentary system is emphasized at the expense of its liberty dimension. Under majority government, parliament as a meaningful forum for the discussion of public affairs virtually disappears; that is why I have argued in earlier chapters for the virtues of minority government. Under minority government, the leaders of the governing party must take parliament seriously *all* the time.

In this final chapter I will turn away from the politicians to that other source of trouble with our parliamentary system— the people. I realize that I am on dangerous ground in taking on "the people." In a democracy, the politicians are fair game; they are open to all kinds of criticism. But the people—the *demos*—can do no wrong. The popular credo is that politicians stink and the people are wonderful. Risky as it may be, my experience in our public life leads me to turn that credo around. Elected politicians, if not quite wonderful, are certainly admirable. The politicians I have known—and I have known many of all political stripes—tend to be well-informed, hard-working, honest people who are public-spirited enough to risk their personal and economic security (and their good name) to run for public office. The people—and I have known many more of them—tend to be ill informed and cynical about politics, preferring to devote their time to the pursuit of their own private interests rather than participating in democratic politics.

When it comes to parliamentary democracy, the great majority of Canadians know very little about the nature of parliamentary government and its virtues. Moreover, the great majority, as I read them, have little regard for the political give-and-take that is crucial for the operation of parliamentary democracy. Parliamentary democracy will be difficult to sustain if these two shortcomings of the *demos*—lack of knowledge about the parliamentary system and a disdain for politics—are not overcome.

The Educational Deficit

I am frequently asked to give lectures on the nature of our parliamentary system and how it differs from the American system of government. What is striking about these invitations is that many of them come from groups composed predominantly of university-educated retirees. These folks are not newcomers to our country—they are well educated and, as voters, they have been "doing" parliamentary democracy for years. Yet it is evident from their questions and note-taking that they know very little about it. Now if that is the case with this group, I would hazard a guess that the level of knowledge about the parliamentary system is even lower among the rest of the population, especially among those who have recently come to Canada and who lack any experience of citizenship in a parliamentary democracy.

The educational deficit when it comes to parliamentary democracy stems in part from the fact that in Canada, as in other countries with parliamentary systems based on the Westminster model, the rules governing the system are not written down in a formal constitutional document. These rules, and the principles underlying them, have evolved through political practice over many generations. They are a part—indeed, the most important part—of our so-called "unwritten constitution." You can skim through the text of our founding Constitution, the Constitution Act, 1867 (formerly known as the British North America Act), and find not one mention of the prime minister or the cabinet, or indeed of the rule—so crucial to the democratic character of our parliamentary system—that the Queen (in whom section 9 of the Constitution vests "The Executive Government of and over Canada") must act on the advice of ministers who have the confidence of the elected house of Parliament. Compare this with the United States, where schoolchildren and newcomers can learn from a short, clear constitutional text the powers of the president and of Congress, how individuals are elected for these positions, and how the positions relate to each other.

The basic rules regulating the operation of the parliamentary system are encoded in the formal constitutions of many parliamentary countries, including the newer parliamentary members of the Commonwealth. There was one attempt in Canada to write some of the key rules of parliamentary government into our "written" Constitution. Bill C-60, a 1978 constitutional proposal of the Trudeau government that aimed at reforming the institutions of federal government, included an effort to codify the basic conventions of responsible government.[2] Australia attempted to do much the same thing through a Constitutional Convention that ran from 1973 to 1985.[3] Both efforts came to naught. Encapsulating in precise legal terms the nuances of political practices and conventions that have evolved over many years is a very tricky business—rather like trying to nail jelly to the wall. It is next to impossible to get experts and politicians to agree on a proper formulation and on how much to cover. Efforts to codify existing rules inevitably arouse interest in *changing* the rules. And, in Canada, there is the added difficulty that any formal constitutional proposal touching the role of the Crown (which the rules of parliamentary government are bound to do) requires not only the approval of the federal Parliament but of all the provincial legislatures as well. For the foreseeable future, we cannot hope to reduce the educational deficit about parliamentary government through constitutional codification—even if we wanted to.

Leaving the rules of parliamentary government in their unwritten form does not mean that they are frozen in time. Quite to the contrary, one of the benefits of informal constitutional rules is that they are able to evolve and adapt to changing circumstances; we are just now witnessing an example of this in the adoption of fixed dates for parliamentary elections. As noted in the previous chapter, one consequence of this change is that, when a Parliament is past its early months but has not run its full course of four years, the Governor General should no longer automatically grant a dissolution to a prime minister whose government has not been defeated on a confidence vote in the House of Commons. Informal constitutional conventions rely on the political process, not the courts, for their interpretation. The weight of effective public opinion is the only sanction for their enforcement. This makes the challenge to civic education in the principles and practices of parliamentary democracy all the more important.

Where can we find this kind of education in Canada? At the university level, political science departments are the principal repositories of teaching and research on parliamentary democracy. Canadian political science was founded by scholars like MacGregor Dawson, James Mallory, and Norman Ward, who gave us lucid written accounts of the background and practice of parliamentary institutions. That tradition has been carried on by a strong contingent of contemporary political scientists, on whose works I have drawn extensively in writing this book. Most political science departments at Canadian universities and colleges have at least one or two faculty members who can provide substantial coverage of parliamentary government and politics in their courses. The same cannot be said for our law schools. There are, to be sure, a few law professors who are knowledgeable about the "unwritten" part of our constitutional system and who discuss it in their writings; professor Peter Hogg's seminal and ongoing work, the *Constitutional Law of Canada*, is a notable example. But the malleable nature of constitutional rules that cannot be looked up in a written text or checked out in the decisions of judges does not fit well with the discipline of law. We will continue to rely primarily on political scientists to pass on the lore of parliamentary government to the future politicians who will practise it, the journalists who will cover it, and the educators who will teach it.

It is in the schools where citizenship is shaped that there is the greatest need to bolster the educational resources of our parliamentary democracy. Here, the need is not only for teachers who are knowledgeable about the workings of our parliamentary institutions, but also for teaching materials that can engage and inform young Canadians in their formative school years. In recent years, the Teachers Institute, a program sponsored by the Library of Parliament, has begun to address this challenge in a systematic way.[4] The Teachers Institute brings teachers to Ottawa for a week to observe Parliament in action and meet with MPs, senators, and parliamentary officials. The 70 or so teachers who participate each year return to their classrooms with a much better grounding in the operation of parliamentary government and armed with materials for communicating this knowledge to their students. In partnership with the Churchill Society for the Advancement of Parliamentary Democracy, the potential of this program has been significantly increased through summer workshops that train teachers to teach other teachers in their locality about parliamentary government. An interactive DVD is being developed that will enable students to participate in classroom simulations of parliamentary debate. In addition, there is a great need to develop materials on parliamentary democracy that are written especially for immigrants preparing for citizenship, and for those teaching English as a second language.

Civic education is of vital importance for sustaining parliamentary democracy. It must be attacked with a sense of urgency. Nothing less than the essential popular foundation of our parliamentary system is at stake.

Appreciating Parliamentary Democracy

If it is important for the people to know something about the rules and structure of the parliamentary system in which they exercise their democratic rights, it is equally important that they have some appreciation of what they know. Here, we encounter another kind of deficit—an enjoyment deficit.

In Canada, as in many of the older democracies, there is evidence of increasing popular dislike of organized partisan politics. Today, nearly two out of every five *registered* voters do not bother to vote in parliamentary elections. Among those *eligible* to vote, the percentage of non-voters may be closer to 50%. As for political parties, the vehicles for aggregating voter preferences and giving expression to them in Parliament, most Canadians would not touch them with a barge pole. According to a recent study, the number of Canadians who report that they have never been members of or worked for a political party has jumped from 74 to 85% in the last three years.[5] Reinforcing the statistical evidence are the snide and cynical remarks I hear every day from anyone with whom I dare talk about politics or about what's going on in Parliament. There is a lot of interest in politics, but most of it is focused on the seamy side of the show— on the misdeeds of government and the foibles of politicians. Moral outrage is the dominant tone of most of the political chit-chat that reaches my ears.

The main reason for all this negativity is that the mass media of communication—the windows through which the people view parliamentary politics—give so much coverage to scandals and screw-ups. It is a rare day when we don't pick up a newspaper or turn on the news and learn about a new mess in Ottawa or a new spin on an old mess. Once news editors get hold of a juicy story about political skullduggery or incompetence, they will wring every drop they can out of it. In an era of "gotcha" journalism, politicians are the hunted and journalists are the hunters, ever on the prowl for the whiff of some political misdeed, off-colour remark, or dubious goings-on. There is nothing new about finding miscreants in government. Great political scandals, from Sir John A. Macdonald's Pacific scandal to Jean Chrétien's sponsorship scandal, drift through our history like crazy floats in a parade. Canadian politicians today are certainly no more corrupt or incompetent than their predecessors. Indeed, because they are held to higher levels of competence and probity, I believe that government and politicians are considerably more competent and honourable today than they were in the past. But now, hunted by a pack of investigative journalists who are aided and abetted by access-to-information laws, politicians and government officials are more exposed than ever before—indeed, their activities are expected to be "transparent"! The other big change is the dominance of television as the media through which most people get most of their news about politics. Television news editors dine out on the ten-second clip of raging faces of people who are fed up and won't put up with it any more. Eyes "glaze over" when the "policy wonks" are given their turn.

There is no point in getting upset about the media. For one thing, they won't change, and for another, they are doing their job. Canada has a strong contingent of journalists who provide insightful analysis of parliamentary affairs and are able to keep the smelly stuff in perspective. Although they do most of their work in the print media, many of them do their share of television and radio. The gotcha journalists—even though they sometimes go over the top and act like a crazed pack of lemmings—*do* contribute to keeping parliamentary government accountable. If you go looking for such journalists in Moscow or Beijing, you had best look in the prisons or graveyards. Here in Canada, there is plenty of good, interesting stuff—beyond the stuff of scandal—about parliamentary life out there in the media and on the Internet for those who have an appetite for it.

One kind of "stuff" that should be a point of interest in following parliamentary affairs is discussion and debate about public policy. Parliament is much more likely to be a forum for such discussion under conditions of minority government, when the government's survival depends on its capacity to take into account views other than its own. This means that the politicians who lead minority government have to modify positions they took in the election campaign or in the early days of government. We have watched Stephen Harper do this in allowing debate on Afghanistan, in keeping some of the Liberals' child-care program, in taking climate change seriously, in softening his get-tough-on-crime proposals, and in his first two budgets. Similarly, opposition leaders have to trim their sails a little and settle for getting modest changes in policy out of the government. Often, however, this give-and-take in policy-making—the life-blood of minority parliaments—is viewed badly by the media and, consequently, is received badly by the public. Compromising or deviating from strong ideological positions is portrayed as showing weakness and lack of principle. Rex Murphy, one of Canada's most influential print and broadcast journalists, commenting on the concessions and accommodations Harper has made, asks: "Is he 'just' a politician after all?"[6] The implication is that strong, principled leaders never waver.

Principles, ideals, and fundamental values have their place in democratic politics—but so does artful compromise. This is especially true in a democracy, where success in ruling depends not only on a leader's partisan supporters but also on the support of partisan *opponents*, and is pre-eminently the situation of government leaders under conditions of minority government. Leaders of minority governments would do well to heed Machiavelli's advice: "For a man who wants to make a profession of good in all regards must come to grief among so many who are not good."[7] Every political party will have its ideologues who feel betrayed when their party's leaders gain power and fail to deliver what they believed their leaders stood for. We have seen that sense of betrayal in the disillusion of Stephen Harper's former soulmates in the National Citizens Coalition. But the National Citizens Coalition could not win office in a small town, let alone in a country with the political diversity of Canada.

In judging politicians, there is a danger in being excessively principled. Important as the principles we believe in and fight for in the politics of our country are, we should have some modesty about them. Our beliefs about what policies will make for a more just, more secure, or more prosperous society are just that—beliefs, not absolute, irrefutable truths. As democratic citizens, we should be prepared to listen to views that challenge our own, and not just tolerate, but *respect*, leaders who work out positions that embrace a larger consensus than that of their most ardent camp followers. To be sure, parliamentary leaders will have to persuade us of the reasons for the accommodations they make. But we should be open to such persuasion and resist the impulse to see every compromise as a mark of weakness. Appreciating parliamentary politics, especially under conditions of minority government, requires a taste for the arts of negotiation and compromise as well as for their fruit.

There are, however, limits to the shifting and changing about that a democratic electorate should tolerate. One of these is the switching of parties by politicians immediately after they are elected. Crossing the floor of the House on a matter of principle or policy is an honourable tradition of parliamentary politics. When an MP is persuaded during the course of a Parliament that on vital issues of policy he or she has come to prefer the position taken on the other side of the aisle, it is a sign that parliamentary debate and discussion are being taken seriously. Winston Churchill, as he said of himself, "ratted" and "re-ratted," but the one time he switched parties during a parliamentary session was early in his career when he found he could no longer support the Tories' protectionist tariff policy and was attracted to the innovative social welfare program of the Liberals. It is quite another thing to switch from one party to another immediately after an election and to be rewarded for this act of blatant voter deception with a cabinet position in the government of a party that was so recently opposed. That is precisely what David Emerson did when, having run as a Liberal in the 2006 election, he accepted an invitation to join the Conservative cabinet immediately following the election. Up until the King–Byng crisis of 1926, Canada followed a convention that required MPs who had never presented themselves to the electorate as ministers to resign and run in a by-election before taking a position in their own party's cabinet. Consideration should be given to reviving that rule for MPs who "pull an Emerson." It would be worth taking a look at the rule being considered in New Zealand (and mentioned in the last chapter) for making party-switching more difficult.

Responsible Government and Deliberative Democracy

The vital first step in turning parliamentary government into democratic government came with the achievement of responsible government. In Canada, that transition occurred in the 1840s, when British governors accepted that, in exercising the executive authority of the Crown, they must act on the advice (that is, the direction) of a council of ministers who have the confidence of the elected legislative assembly. With that change in place, government was no longer responsible and accountable to the Crown, but to the people's representatives assembled in Parliament. When parliamentary government is equated with responsible government, parliament's role is conceived of primarily in terms of holding the government accountable and enabling an alternative government to make its case. That conception of parliamentary government minimizes parliament's role in legislation and policy-making. In the words of C.E.S. Franks, a leading expositor of the classical Westminster parliamentary model:

> Parliamentary activities of legislating and policy-making are largely aspects of the function of making government work, and parliament's role in them is not now, nor has it ever been, the dominant one.[8]

The liberty element in this view of parliamentary democracy rests largely on the free, competitive elections that determine which group of politicians will direct government.

Responsible government is an important rationale for parliamentary government. Holding ministers to account for what the departments and agencies of government have done—or not done—continues to be a major function of parliament, though one not easily discharged when government has become so enormous and ministers so adroit at taking the credit for what has gone right while refusing to accept personal responsibility for what has gone wrong. But responsible government is not the only normative rationale for the parliamentary system.

There is another tradition of parliamentary government that emphasizes parliament's role as a national forum where the great issues of the day are debated and government becomes possible through free and civilized discussion. It was this aspect of parliamentary government that the Olympian parliamentarian Winston Churchill valued so much; in fact, it was his reason for making sure that the British House of Commons sat regularly and debated policy throughout the Second World War. In the words of Martin Gilbert, Churchill's biographer:

> An essential part of Churchill's concept of parliamentary democracy was his belief that nothing, even in the bitterest political controversy, must be allowed to damage the fabric of peaceful debate and civilized discourse.[9]

In the depth of the war, Ernest Barker gave a more philosophical account of parliament's value as a forum for government by discussion:

> If a majority engages in discussion with a minority, and if that discussion is conducted in a spirit of giving and taking, the result will be that the ideas of the majority are widened to include some of the ideas of the minority which have established their truth in the give and take of debate.[10]

When parliament is thought of in this way, its role in policymaking and legislation is not simply to enable the government—be it a majority or minority—to govern, but for its members (including its non-governmental members) to participate in enacting laws and shaping policy.

Contemporary democratic theorists have developed a fancier, more sophisticated justification of government by discussion.

They call it deliberative democratic theory.[11] Deliberative democratic theory emphasizes the communicative processes of democracy, rather than simply the power of numbers. Government decisions become legitimate not because the side with the most votes has made them, but because they are made in a way that enables the great body of citizens to feel that they participated in the decision-making. This form of democratic decision-making is called "deliberation," and is described by Simone Chambers as "debate and discussion aimed at producing reasonable, well-informed opinions in which participants are willing to revise preferences in the light of discussion, new information, and claims made by fellow participants."[12]

When parliamentary government is thought of normatively as aspiring to both responsible government and deliberative democracy, a broader understanding of its service to liberty opens up. Parliamentary government provides for liberty not only by making government responsible to the representatives of the majority, but also by conducting its business in a manner that gives all citizens a sense that their views and interests were taken into account in its decisions. When parliament provides for this deliberative possibility, there is a greater likelihood that citizens will experience the liberal ideal of being subject to laws they make for themselves. This is the quality of liberty that Alexis de Tocqueville, that great chronicler of liberty, so eloquently described when he asked:

> Is any man born with a soul so base as to prefer to depend on the whims of someone like himself rather than obey laws he has helped to establish, if his nation appears to have the virtue necessary to make a right use of liberty?[13]

Deliberative democracy is, of course, an ideal that is only partially realized in the politics of a representative democracy like Canada. Much of its realization occurs in the formation of opinion that takes place in the pre-voting stages of democratic politics. But if we are to aspire seriously to the ideal of deliberative democracy—as I think we should—it must have some reality in the institution we create through our voting: Parliament. The fundamental argument of this book is that the prospect of this happening in Parliament is greatest when we have a minority government. For then, and only then, the government of the day has no choice—the arithmetic of survival requires the inclusion of more than its own views in making laws and policy. To be sure, deliberative democracy—government by discussion—is important in parliamentary life whether a government has a majority or a minority. But efficiency and liberty, the virtues of parliamentary democracy, will be in better balance when no single political party has a majority in the House of Commons.

It may well be that many who read this book do not need to be persuaded that minority government is worth at least two cheers. Thirty years ago, political scientist Larry LeDuc analyzed the state of public opinion in Canada on minority government.[14] LeDuc found that when asked whether they preferred majority to minority government, a majority (55%) favoured majority government. But when he dug deeper, LeDuc found considerable support for minority government. A survey conducted after the 1974 election reported that a majority thought the Trudeau minority government had been "good for the nation."[15] LeDuc also found that, for most voters, whether an election produced a majority or a minority government was not an important issue. People generally were not inclined to vote strategically to either provide or deny a majority to any party.

Today, as we watch the Harper minority government, I have a sense that there is at least as much popular support for minority government as there was 30 years ago. Harper's personality as presented to us by the media may well be a factor. "What would he be like if he had a majority?" I hear people ask with a tremor of fear in their voice. It augurs well for sustaining parliamentary democracy if Canadians vote for the party or candidate of their choice without heeding the pleas of party leaders that they must have a majority. I promise to vote that way myself—though I must confess that my spirits will soar if our next federal election produces a minority Parliament.

Notes

1. See José Antonio Cheibub, *Presidentialism, Parliamentarism, and Democracy* (New York: Cambridge University Press, 2007).

2. *The Constitutional Amendment Bill: Text and Explanatory Notes* (Ottawa: Government of Canada, 1978).

3. See Peter H. Russell, "The Politics of Frustration: The Pursuit of Formal Constitutional Change in Australia and Canada," *Australian Canadian Studies* 3 (1988): 3–32.

4. Information about the Teachers Institute is available at www.parl.gc.ca/information/about/education.

5. *News—Canadians Distrust Government, Embrace Volunteerism* (Montreal: Trudeau Foundation, November 11, 2005). I am indebted to Donald Savoie for this reference. For a comparative analysis of this and other evidence of Canadians' disenchantment with politics, see Donald Savoie, *The Return of Court Government, The Decline of Bureaucracy and the Fall of Accountability: Canada and the UK* (Toronto: University of Toronto Press, forthcoming).

6. Rex Murphy, "Cabinet change: Why shuffle straw men?" *Globe and Mail*, August 18, 2007, A19.

7. Niccolò Machiavelli, *The Prince*, translated with an introduction by Harvey C. Mansfield (Chicago: University of Chicago Press, 1985), 61. For a discussion of the positive role hypocrisy can play in politics, see Ruth W. Grant, *Hypocrisy and Integrity: Machiavelli, Rousseau, and the Ethics of Politics* (Chicago: University of Chicago Press, 1997).

8. C.E.S. Franks, *The Parliament of Canada* (Toronto: University of Toronto Press, 1987), 5.

9. Martin Gilbert, *The Will of the People: Winston Churchill and Parliamentary Democracy* (Toronto: Vintage Canada, 2006), 47.

10. Ernest Barker, *Reflections on Government* (Oxford: Oxford University Press, 1942).

11. There are many contributors to this school. The German political philosopher Jurgen Habermas is usually regarded as its founder. For a good summary and analysis, see Simone Chambers, "Deliberative Democratic Theory," *American Review of Political Science* 6 (2003): 307–26.

12. Ibid., 309.

13. Quoted in Hugh Brogan, *Alexis de Tocqueville: A Life* (New Haven, CT: Yale University Press, 2006), 567.

14. Lawrence LeDuc, "Political Behavior and the Issue of Majority Government," *Canadian Journal of Political Science* 10 (1977): 311–39.

15. Ibid., 313.

Index